PATH
TO PROFIT

A Trader's Journey

GEORGE PAPAZOV

George Papazov
TRADEPRO Publishing
TRADEPRO Academy Inc

Printed in the United States of America
First Printing 2019
First Edition 2019
ISBN: 978-1-7770500-0-9

10 9 8 7 6 5 4 3 2 1

If you want to get a copy of the Path to Profit workbook and some free training resources that have helped me immensely, visit our website:
www.pathtoprofitbook.com

PATH
TO PROFIT

Acknowledgements

First and foremost, I want to thank the universe for giving me this miracle called life. It is calculated that the odds of receiving the gift of life is equivalent to two million people in one room, each holding a dice of one billion sides - and hitting the same number!

Now imagine the odds you are reading this book I have written. Thank you universe; for the love, abundance, power, strength, passion and purpose. I love you. I will continue to serve you.

To my wife, Reese, I can write a Harry Potter volume of books about how much I love you, and I would still have only scratched the surface. You have believed in me from day one, and supported me through all the tough times. I cherish every moment and memory we share. Thank you for starting me on this journey of personal development and pushing me to get certified as a master practitioner of NLP. It has changed my life. I love you so much, and constantly more with each passing day.

Also, I want to thank my parents for their sacrifice. The courage to leave everything behind in search for a better life is my inspiration to push through the hard times. I love you both more than words can express, in either English or Bulgarian. I also want to send love to my sister and her beautiful family, to my brother-in law Brad and my nieces; Mikael and Alyssa. I love you all. Thank you so much.

I want to thank Stephen Box, who put up with me through the editing process of my first book. With few words you have the gift of communicating a universe of meaning. Thank you for giving your time and energy to myself, and the entire TRADEPRO community. You are truly an amazing soul, and I am so thankful I have the pleasure of calling you my friend, and one of the greatest crude oil traders that ever lived. Put in a good word for me to Crudella.

I also want to acknowledge and thank my good friend Anthony Drager, who introduced me to the world of order flow trading in futures. I've learned a lot from you, and it's an honor to call you my friend. I always look forward to our accountability chats, and brainstorming new ideas on how to innovate and steer the future course of our industry. I'm really excited for the next chapter of our collaboration and friendship. Thank you for being a great friend and mentor.

Lastly, but not least, I want to thank each and every TRADEPRO in our community. You are all my family. Waking up every morning to trade with you is a blessing I am grateful for. When you succeed, you motivate me beyond belief. You are the jet fuel for my creative soul. Let's keep succeeding, striving for more and helping others achieve their dreams.

I have a lot more people to thank, because my success is a collective effort of everyone I have ever met.

I thank you all for your help and support over the years; what a beautiful journey we are on.

Love you all immensely.

TABLE OF CONTENTS

PREFACE

This book took me over thirty years to write. I wrote this to tell my story, as a story is the most powerful teacher. But more importantly, I wanted you to learn more about trading and to be able to use my nearly twenty years of experience as a tool to create your own story.

The purpose of this book is to give you inspiration, and to learn from my twists and turns so you can travel a more direct path than I did. And as you will find out, my flight path was everything but direct.

The first few chapters are detailed events of my life, as I progressed from an immigrant to Canada to a professional trader at one of the biggest banks.

At the end of every chapter, there will be an exercise to help you reflect and craft what your journey will look like. They say to learn the most, you have to ask the best questions. I ask you my best questions; those that have caused the biggest changes in the thousands of traders I have worked with in the last eighteen years.

In the last few chapters, I lay out the framework for you to develop a success mindset and provide exercises to help you do it. You will get an actionable nine-day plan that will change the course of your life. The most important part of achieving success is to start thinking successfully.

You will then learn one of the most common pitfalls that cause traders to fail, and how to avoid it so you can get started the right way. The sad part is most traders that fail never gave themselves a chance to succeed; you will.

The book then concludes with a detailed list of lessons I have learned from my trading career at the bank, to the transition of entrepreneurship. Also, I will share my biggest lessons of life in general, designed to shift your thinking and get you firing on all cylinders.

We conclude with a final chapter, which lays out the steps for getting started as a new trader. If I could give a plan to the younger me in 2001 when I started this crazy journey, what would it be? What would be the most important steps to succeed as a trader today?

In a way, this book is part story and part self-development. You get to experience my journey while simultaneously creating the blueprint for what you want yours to look like.

It is a book of learning, which itself created many learnings in the process.

You are getting an inside look into my life, my past, present and my future plans. You will experience my thoughts, emotions and vulnerabilities and have massive takeaways for yourself.

This book is all about being raw, unfiltered and uncut. While this book is written by me, it is entirely for you and designed to create lasting change.

As you read each chapter, you will find some very powerful exercises. I strongly suggest getting a notebook handy to record your progress and to complete the exercises.

Now, let's take a journey of self-discovery and reflection together.

To begin, we will start with the beginning itself, and how I got into the trading industry.

CHAPTER 1
HOW I GOT INTO TRADING

My life changed forever on October 19th of 1993 at 10PM. This is the day our family immigrated to Toronto, Canada from Bulgaria. The night that we arrived we slept on the waiting benches at the Toronto Pearson arrivals terminal. As a seven year old kid, it seemed exciting and like a world of new opportunity opening up.

For my parents, I'm sure the feeling was different. They packed their bags and left everything behind to move to a foreign country in search of a better life. Everything we had known and owned changed overnight.

The sacrifice they made for our family is something I am grateful for, and that I owe the success of my life to.

As far back as I can remember, I have always wanted to be successful. Maybe it was to make my parents proud. Maybe it was because it was necessary to pay the bills. But success in my mind was not about if it would happen, just a matter of when and how.

I worked many jobs in my early teenage years. I started with a paper route on Sunday mornings. During the weekday evenings I also had an office cleaning job where I held the prestigious job of cleaning the toilets. I eventually earned a promotion and started throwing out the trash. No matter what I was doing, I was working as hard as I could and aimed to be the best.

Then I built and operated a music recording studio in my bedroom, where I also engineered and mastered music. On the side I created mix CD's for kids in my high school, downloading the songs they wanted and putting them on one piece of recordable media. At the time, this was revolutionary. My backpack was stuffed with so many CDs I had to leave my textbooks at home. As far back as I can remember I was always wheeling and dealing, and looking for the next hustle.

Since immigrating to Canada in 1993, my parents were constantly in between jobs and always looking for work. They needed experience to get a job in their field, but had a hard time gaining that experience without a job. The Catch 22.

Both of my parents were very well educated and left behind great careers in Bulgaria. Even though it put a lot of stress on them, they were very strong and enforced our family values. They did their best to provide for us. They were a big source of motivation and inspiration for me to succeed in life, although I know at the time it was very difficult for them to adapt to the Western culture.

This frustration pushed my father, a computer engineer, to look for a different way to generate income to support his family. He found currency trading and my calling in life at the same time.

In 2001, at the age of 16, my father made me a simple proposition. I can give you a fish, or teach you how to fish. Do you want a small weekly allowance, or to learn how to trade?

To this day, it remains the easiest choice I've ever made.

I was really excited to learn that I could make money working at home on the computer. I could make my own schedule, be my own boss and be a productive member of our family. This was far more lucrative than cleaning toilets and burning CDs. While music was still a big passion and dream for me, it was now not the only option. It was a moment of great awakening.

This was the second time my life changed forever. The door to the rest of my life opened and I stepped in with a smile on my face.

This was the day I assumed my identity of who I am to this very moment.

I became a trader.

From that moment, I split all of my spare time between learning about trading and pursuing a career in music. Deep down, my intuition kept sending me subtle messages that one of these would be my ticket out of being broke. It would be my ticket to everything I have ever wanted.

I started to read as much information as I could that year. From books at the local library, to online articles and everything in between. At school during class, I remember having a trading book inside my textbook - so I could learn what I was really passionate about. I really don't think I was getting away with it, but my teacher was just happy to see me so eager to learn and let it slide.

Learning to trade at that time was a very different experience than it is today.

In the early 2000's there was a limited amount of knowledge on the internet. It was the age of the dial up connection and every website looked like a Wikipedia page. There was no YouTube and very little video content existed due to the slow internet speeds. Only 7% of internet users worldwide had broadband connections. The other 93%

had to choose between using the internet or their landline phones. I remember searching for trading articles online, while my sister would yell at me to get off the phone as she's been trying to call her friend for hours.

In the trading industry, newspapers were still printing daily quotes and charts in the finance section. It was particularly challenging to go from reading about trading strategies to visually seeing how they were applied on the limited charting software that was available. It was truly a time of self-teaching.

What I do remember is the volatility that started in 2001. I was spoiled with opportunity which I could not fully appreciate in that moment. This was my first taste of trading and how I cut my teeth.

The Euro was trading around $0.87 to the US dollar, while the SP500 stock market was in the process of imploding as the Dot Com bubble burst with fierceness.

I was still trading in a simulated account under my dad's name with an FX broker by the name of Oanda. Since I was not yet at the age of majority and could not open my own account, I experienced the biggest volatility in a decade in a simulated account.

My strategy was simple, keep buying Euros vs USD on retracements to the support line, and watch the US dollar slump on a fire sale.

I became a simulated millionaire. The profits were fake, yet the learning was priceless.

This obviously did not stop me from looking at Ferraris and Lamborghinis on the internet, all loading horizontally with the type of slowness typical of the dial up internet era.

During this time, I was also beginning to work with a lot of promising artists in the music industry in Toronto - some of which have very successful careers today.

I remember spending three weeks researching on how to build the perfect home studio. One weekend I went to the local hardware store and purchased a few pieces of plywood, glue and a mattress comforter from a home decor store nearby. I had to soundproof the recording room on a really tight budget. As soon as I returned from the store, I went straight to work. Within a few hours I put together a booth that would serve as our recording studio for almost a year. It looked like a boarded up home with all the plywood, but the sound quality was really good for the money it cost to build.

Everyone in our neighborhood was empowered, because they had a place to share their message. The effort paid off; as the studio gave a lot of people a voice, and it was one of the first times I got to experience the joy of helping others. It was a dream factory. But the problem was that it was also causing a lot of traffic in our home, and it really wasn't the optimal place for a business that needed to scale. The early success and the caliber of music that was coming out of this home project really inspired me. I saw the vision for what it could become.

My love for music grew at an equal pace to my love for trading.

The next few years of my life would become a tug of war between my two loves.

CHAPTER EXERCISE

Trading for me became about finding a way out of a troubled neighborhood. I grew up around trading, and matured because of the opportunity of trading. Having something so inspirational in my life kept me off the streets. My purpose was to create a better life for myself and to help my family. Trading was my means of survival.

Before you begin anything, it is important to know what you want to accomplish, so you can set your GPS to steer you to your goal. Start with the end goal in mind.

Now here are some questions to answer for yourself. Grab a pen and a coffee and let's get to work!

- What is your reason for wanting to trade?
- Who are you trading for?
- What kind of lifestyle do you want to live as a trader?
- How much money do you want to make? (not how much you need, but how much do you WANT).
- What will you do with the money?
- How will you give back?
- What does a day in the life of a successful trader look like for you?

Now that you know what you are doing this for, you'll have a vision to return to when times get hard and something to celebrate when times are great.

CHAPTER 2
MAJOR SETBACK AND A SMALL WIN

I n the summer of 2002 a really good friend of mine named Allen made a very bold move that changed the course of my life. Allen was a colleague at the retail flooring store I worked at part time. He also attended the same high school as me and we shared a passion of eventually running a successful independent music label. I was also one of the artists on our roster, but there is zero chance you have heard any of the songs. I plan to keep it this way forever for a very personal reason which I will get to.

The music industry was at its height during this time, with compact disc sales peaking in 2000 and total music revenues exceeding $21 billion dollars. Music was still profitable, and we had a very talented group of artists working with us. For those that don't remember, CD's were round plastic things that could hold up to a whopping twenty songs. It was anything but portable.

In realizing our opportunity, Allen took a big step, and cashed out his college savings to help us setup a professional recording studio with top notch industry equipment. I tried to talk him out of this idea initially, but he was the only person that I knew who was more stubborn than me. I thought we could start smaller and scale up. He really didn't ask for permission from anyone, he just did as he pleased. So the studio was built, and it was completed very quickly.

This was great news to my mom, as it meant we could move our studio out of my bedroom. I know she was happy for both of us; for me because I was chasing a dream and also for the return of her quiet days at home.

Everything was going amazing with music, and trading took a back seat during this time. I was still checking the charts daily, but it just wasn't a focus for me. I knew I could pick up trading at any time in my career, while the music business was a young man's game and I felt like I was getting older. I look back at this idea of "getting older" and laugh today, the same way I'm sure I'll do a few decades from now about this moment.

This was our shot, it was our time. The grit in me was ready to get to the top, and anything less would be a failure.

I read through countless books on the music business. Talented artistry is great, but the music business is more about business than it is about music. This is true to this day. I read through information as feverishly as I did on trading just a year earlier.

Everyone at the label was making amazing music and it was just a matter of time before we got our big shot.

Over the next year we produced our best music and spent every hour outside of school and work locked up in the studio.

As fall was approaching in 2003, Allen and I went to look at a new car he was thinking of buying. I remember this moment with crystal clarity, down to every word of the conversation.

Everything about the car was amazing, yet for some reason I had a feeling that something was not right. It had low kilometers, it was well maintained, stylish and at a great price. Yet, something about it felt off. But because I did not know how to express my inner feelings and did not want to hurt his, I went along with it and supported my friend with his decision. He bought the car the next day.

Not speaking up on this day is one of my biggest regrets.

On December 17th in 2003, Allen called me offering to pick me up so we can drive to work together. It was cold outside in Scarborough and he is the type to offer his help graciously at every chance.

I told Allen I was already on my way to work on public transit and that I would see him when I got there. He told me he made a song that he wanted me to listen to, then we said goodbye and hung up the phone.

This was the last time I got to speak with Allen.

On his drive in to work that evening, Allen got into a tragic car accident that took his life.

When I walked into work, I saw the entire staff in a huddle and I will never forget the look on their faces. It was a look of disappointment, a silent despair that gave me chills. I immediately knew something bad had happened. I really don't remember much during the first hour that followed, except that I went to the lunchroom and cried for the first time since I was a child.

When my adrenaline decreased a little, I called a friend who told me the accident happened in front of his house. He lived approximately three kilometers away from where we worked. I started running in the cold towards his house, leaving my jacket behind at work.

I'm not really sure what I was expecting to see, but I was not prepared for what I saw. A tow truck was in the process of hooking up Allen's car and emergency workers were cleaning up the scene. The ambulance had already taken Allen and his passenger to the hospital.

I remember seeing a knocked-over hydro pole, a crowd of people and an oil slick that ran down the decline of the road for at least ten meters.

In that very moment, time seemed to stop. As I stared at Allen's Celica, lying upside down on its roof, I thought to myself - you should have said something. I was in complete shock and disbelief, and couldn't help but wonder who was in the passenger seat. Who was in the seat that I so frequently sat in?

I found out the passenger was a mutual friend of ours, and he was in critical condition but was expected to survive. Because the oxygen was cut off to his brain due to the seat-belt strangling him while the car was upside down - the doctors did not expect a full recovery. They were right, Chris also passed away a few months after the accident.

Every year on December 17th, I go to the crash site and do a meditation to send both of their families and friends, love, joy, healing energy and happiness. The oil slick on the road is still there sixteen years later.

The months following the accident are still a blur. When I try to recall the sequence of events they are always in a different order, as if though it was a hazy dream without a clear timeline.

No matter how hard I tried to press forward, nothing was the same. The music, the business, the passion - they were all anchored to a painful event I had not yet accepted. It was a dark few months.

It took me years of battling with my love of music after this day to come to a realization that I have never shared with anyone before.

On Wednesday December 17th, 2003 at approximately 7:30PM EST my music ambitions died along with Allen.

Many of the friends and colleagues in our circle went on to have successful music and film careers, and it fills my heart with joy. For me it became the abrupt end of a chapter in the beginning of a book.

After months of drifting aimlessly and getting into trouble, I got used to my new reality of having a life outside the studio. My motivation started to increase again as I thought about Allen's hyper positive attitude. What would he say? Most likely something along the lines of, "get your ass to work man, what are you doing"? The title of one of our favorite songs came to mind, and I remembered that "we will always make it."

I began trading again and had a renewed drive to make as much money as possible and start a studio in his honor. To this day it has not yet happened, but there are future plans for a charity studio to provide youth in lower economic neighborhoods a voice. Every time I'm around musical equipment, I experience a raw energy of sorts that I cannot find the words to describe.

My return to music is inevitable at some point, but this time just as a hobby and a way to give back. Music changed my life, and I plan to spread this gift to others when my intuition sends me a message that it's time.

I began to feel joy and excitement for trading again and I opened and funded an account under my own name. I was ready to take on the world and to achieve my wildest dreams.

I started trading the XAU/USD pair, which is a Contract for Difference (CFD) investment vehicle that lets you bet on the price of gold without owning it. In addition to this I was trading most major currency pairs and a few of the minors.

As my performance increased, my passion ballooned which further enhanced my performance. I got into a groove. I felt the same flow I used to when I was in the studio.

My high school friend Guggan was also trading currencies at the time and we held weekly meetings to talk about market conditions, and our trading game plan.

We built a great relationship over the span of a few short months and decided to partner up and fund an account with our own capital. He traded currencies and I traded gold. We started a prop trading firm in our late teenage years.

Our plans were to grow our account and fund traders with the proceeds. I was also drafting up the concept of institutional services to hedge currency exposure for medium sized businesses. This idea was ahead of the time for me, as the few businesses I pitched it to had the same feedback: You are too young. I always wondered to myself, too young for what exactly? I couldn't imagine someone that could outwork me, but my take away was that whatever I was doing was not enough. It was time to turn it up a notch.

This was exactly the kind of motivation I needed at the time, and it fueled my desire to succeed beyond what people thought was possible for a kid in my neighborhood. I didn't have a lot of money in my account, but I made up for it with my insane optimism and wild dreams. To me all that mattered is what I could have, and not what I did have. I felt like my mindset was mismatched to my surroundings. This made me feel different all throughout my high school years. But I knew it was a good different.

Guggan and I continued to trade together for several months, and became really good friends in the process. Eventually our paths started to lead us into different directions and we decided to go back to trading on our own. We had our own strategies and a different vision of where it was we were trying to go. In retrospect, this seems like a normal thing for two teenagers.

We held our weekly meetings until eventually, those too stopped and we fell out of touch. I really hope he is doing well today; he is a fantastic person.

I continued to trade gold and the Euro vs the US dollar by myself. Things were going good, I was earning consistently small returns in my account and building up my confidence.

Life was boring again, in a good way. For the first time in a year, I felt alive.

My massive aspirations for self-employment were contrasted to what other kids my age were doing. They were all in college and working towards their careers. Entrepreneurship at the time was still viewed as a bit of an insane decision. The societal template dictated a career was the next step. People got jobs, a regular paycheck and were loyal to their employers. If you worked hard for long enough, you got to retire in forty years and enjoy your freedom.

The world is really different today, and I think the acceptance of entrepreneurship has created some amazing innovations that have improved our lives significantly. We have never had access to so much information and convenience than we do today.

But in those days, my plans stuck out like a sore thumb. Everyone I respected was pointing me in the same direction - college.

My parents supported me with every decision I ever made, for which I love them immensely. My dad loved trading so he understood the potential. My mom was really advocating for me to go to college and find a normal job after I graduate. She wanted me to have a security blanket in case trading failed.

At that time, believe it or not, I had never considered that as an outcome. Not once. Was failure possible I wondered?

I was at a crossroads yet again.

So I took a piece of paper out and on the top I wrote PRO's and CON's.

Directly below I wrote my three options - trading, college and.... you guessed it - music!

CHAPTER EXERCISE

There is a saying: In life you make a plan so you know what isn't going to happen. I have learned this to be true. In trading, plans are necessary to help you manage risk and to quantify your edge. You definitely need a plan. It is also important, however, to consider how you will deal with adverse conditions in both your trading and other aspects of life. Most of us only consider these outcomes when it's too late and when our emotions are high.

So let's start by taking an inventory of our trading intentions. The first set of questions are designed to help you clear your motivation for starting to trade, and to consider your opportunity cost. Any time you choose something, you are also choosing to not choose something else.

You want to get into a quiet space where you can think without interruption, and use a pen and pad to complete this exercise.

Answer these questions with the first thing that comes to mind. Instead of using your logic and thinking brain, go with the answer that is intuitive (your gut feeling):

- What would happen if you started trading?
- What wouldn't happen if you started trading?
- What would happen if you didn't start trading?
- What wouldn't happen if you didn't start trading?

Now let's take some time and create your comeback plan so we can deal with any setbacks that may occur:

- What potential threats could cause you a setback in trading? (List them all)
- How will you deal with a setback in trading?
- What will have to happen such that you temporarily stop trading?
- What resources do you have to help you fix the problem?
- What resources will you need to help you fix the problem?
- How will you know you have fixed the problem?
- What actions will you take to avoid this problem from occurring again?
- What will you do to transition back into trading?
- Who will you turn to as your support partner when you need help or feedback?

CHAPTER 3
CAREER CHANGES

In the summer of 2004 I felt the sudden emotional drain of fighting the current. My trading was focused on longer term swing trades, while I spent most of my days working at an electronics retail store in the computer department.

I felt like I was drifting in the wind, like I had a plan, yet I was choosing to be a part of someone else's instead. My biggest accomplishment in the last few months was being the first representative to sell a VOIP phone (internet phone) in the entire country.

In that year I also started a computer repair business and managed to get a few clients that just made it worth the effort. I learned to build custom computers from my dad, who was an engineer before he moved our family to Canada. Making money from the business was a secondary gain, as the real joy for me was spending quality time with him. But one or two repairs a month wasn't going to fund my big dreams.

Over the years I'd held a lot of different jobs and hustles, but what I really wanted was a career. Painting apartments with my father, mowing lawns, buying and reselling phones and anything else that I could mark up. It made money, and mostly it made me want to find something to settle into.

Luckily, as a trader I always valued the benefit of hedging your bets, and keeping multiple options open.

Earlier in the year I had applied to a few colleges with very little expectations of being accepted. It was a longshot. My high school grades were just good enough to graduate. It wasn't that I didn't care, it was because I was too busy scheming and planning in class for what I would do when I got out of class. My economics professor once told me he was disappointed in my barely passing test score, and that I could do much better. I shared that it was the most efficient grade one can strive for, at least from a return on time spent studying. That was my impression of high school, it felt like a roadblock to my dream life.

And now that I was finally in the workforce full time and had barely graduated, it felt like school was done forever.

Then one day I received an envelope in the mail, which was still pretty common. To my surprise it was an acceptance letter for an Electro-Mechanical Engineering Technology program at Durham College. Basically, robotics.

My father was an engineer and so was my uncle. Was it my turn?

I thought long and hard about what I wanted to do. I really can't pinpoint the decision making factor today, but I accepted the offer. Maybe it was my mom's encouragement and comments that I was good with computers. Or that my friend was also accepted in the same program and he was very excited for both of us. I was interested in technology. But overall I think I was just exhausted from fighting the system and trying to do everything on my own.

The first year of the program was a big adjustment period for me. I took two buses and two trains to travel ninety minutes each way to class. Every day I spent a total of three hours commuting. This was great, because it gave me time to study and finish all my assignments.

Also, it is the reason why my writing is a little messy; there were a lot of turns and bumps along the route. I was very grateful for the financial support of my parents, who sacrificed everything for me to have this opportunity. So I took it in stride.

In the second year, I decided to apply for a student loan so I could live on residence. Also, this became the second worst financial decision I have ever made. Everything changed. I felt immense pressure for having to return large sums of money that I hadn't earned yet.

My focus decreased drastically, and I began to spend an increasing amount of time trading in the computer lab. I missed a lot of classes, yet I found a way to pass my way through the first semester. Once again, I found the perfect balance between just getting the job done with minimal effort invested.

The second semester was full of lab experiments and intensive assignments. My lack of dedication started to reflect in my grades. Towards the end of the semester it was apparent I was going to fail my fluid mechanics class, which would set me back almost an entire year as it was a major prerequisite for the third year of the program.

Once the school year finished a few weeks later, I packed my bags and went home. I would never return to finish the third and final year.

The worst part of it all was the debt I racked up living on campus and paying the school fees. But the best part was that I met the girl that later became my wife in the second year of the program. I am willing to bet that this will go down as the best investment in my life.

That summer I worked a retail job at a sports store in the hard goods department. I continued to trade in the currency markets with a longer term approach, riding trends for days to weeks at a time. In the evenings I thought long and hard about my next move, because I knew it had to be the right one.

One thing was common in every job I worked, or business venture I started: I loved the business of everything. It fascinated me that if you knew how to run a business, you could be in any industry you wanted. When you go to school to learn a craft, you end up getting a job. But when you go to school for business, you can create your job.

When I researched business programs I was intrigued by financial planning, because I would get to learn about personal finance and business at the same time. It sparked a flame inside of me that still burns bright today.

I applied for college for the second time in 2006 a few days before the cut off. Just weeks later I was thrilled to open another acceptance letter.

Everything felt right, it felt congruent. I was more excited about this than anything else up to that point in my life, even music. In that very moment, school became my hustle. My economics teacher would have been really proud.

My first two years of my second attempt at college were incredible. I experienced what it was like to study out of passion, versus necessity. I stayed in school late hours working on economic papers, financial plans and planning my trades. Trading helped my school, and school helped my trading. As a result, I traded with confidence and did very well for myself.

One day sticks out in my memory during my college experience. I closed out a huge win on a trade during a washroom break from my economics exam. On this day I crossed a significant milestone on my trading account and achieved my best mark ever on an exam. I didn't have to wait for the grade to come back--I knew I got a near perfect mark. When you've lived twenty four years of life and have had nearly as many jobs, economics just made practical sense.

That year I joined a student organization that volunteered to help grassroot businesses with their business plans, and I became the president in a few short months. The purpose of the organization was to create measurable change and compete against other schools in front of industry executive judges. Every massive corporation was either a sponsor of this event, or their C-suite executives were on the panel. We won second place in a regional competition against top business schools we had no business beating. I was very proud of the entire team.

In the following year we had to complete a mandatory co-op term for school. Our guidance counsellor told us about a customer service position at Scotiabank's self-directed trading department. I had to get that job I thought, so I applied knowing it would be very competitive.

In a few days I got a call for a phone interview. They asked a few simple questions, after which I had the feeling that it was over and I would never hear back. I hadn't yet learned the poker face interviewing techniques of the corporate world.

A few days later the phone rang again and I was invited for an in person interview in two days. When I walked into the building for an interview I felt a rush of excitement the moment I opened the door. As we walked to the interview room I heard the phones buzzing with conversation that made sense to me. Limit orders, stop losses, option exercises - everything that was in my dreams was right in front of me. I was looking around with my jaw dropped.

During the interview, I had no idea how I was doing. I was just happy to spend another minute in the trading floor environment. I asked a few questions I had prepared, and then a few more I made up just so I could stay a while longer. Towards the end of the meeting, one of the interviewers told me he was going to Europe in three weeks and asked me where to place his sell limit to get the best price on the conversion. With no hesitation whatsoever, I told him a price down to the pip, which is 0.0001 of price move on the Eur vs USD. This was my wheelhouse, I've traded this same asset thousands of times. He tried to seem unphased, but I knew he was impressed.

Three days later in June of 2009 came the call that officially got me started in the professional trading business, where I am to this day.

Walter, one of the interviewers and my future manager asked me if I would accept the customer service position. Before he could finish his sentence I said YES. I hung up the phone in disbelief, in shock and awe.

All of the trials and tribulations, every moment of every minute of my life was made whole in that second. It was a very emotional moment for me to finally integrate my life long passion of trading with a stable career. For once I didn't have to choose! All roads merged into one right there, and it felt incredible.

I was overwhelmed, and for the first time since being at the scene of Allen's crash, I cried. But this time, these were tears of joy.

This time I knew it was the start of something that would last a long time.

Ideally, forever.

CHAPTER EXERCISE

My challenge in my early years was not pursuing my true passion of trading. The decision to take the safe route resulted in a big debt load and an inefficient use of my time. It was not a waste, as I learned a lot about myself and I got the living on campus college experience, which was fun.

If you are a student, I strongly suggest finishing your college program. The most important thing I learned was how to learn, and it gave me the discipline and maturity to excel in my trading as well. The markets are not going anywhere, and you can learn to navigate them while you are in school without the added pressure of doing it for a living.

If you are in a career at the moment and thinking of switching over to trading, I've come up with a few questions to get you thinking deeper into this topic. The choice is personal, and only you will know the right time. The most important part is knowing your reason, your motivators and creating an actionable transition plan.

- What aspects of trading are exciting to you?
- What aspect of trading are not desirable to you?
- Do you want to trade for a side income or as a career?
- Review the answers to the questions in chapter 2. Are you willing to fight through any obstacles to achieve your goals?
- What are you giving up in your current career to pursue trading?
- What is your freedom day? When do you plan to make a career change?

- How will you transition to trading as a career? Will it be part-time at first or will you jump into it full-time?
- What resources do you have to support your new career?
- What resources will you need?

GEORGE PAPAZOV

CHAPTER 4
FIRST STEPS IN THE PROFESSIONAL TRADING WORLD

I will always remember the first day I walked onto the trading floor. It was a melodic hum of conversation. As I walked through the cubicles, it was as if everything was moving in slow motion. All my senses were heightened and I was not just seeing the environment, I was feeling it. Like the warmth of sitting at the dinner table with people you love dearly. I instantly belonged here.

The first three weeks of my job involved intense training. It was customer service, but you had to know most of the same information as traders. It was a steep learning curve for my fellow trainees, but for me it was a matter of knowing the systems. The trading knowledge was mostly a refresher. All the trainees received one massive five inch binder jam packed with paper. This was one of many folders. While the reading seemed boring and dry to my fellow trainees, I took the binder home daily and read ahead with joy and enthusiasm. This was my dream, I was ecstatic to be there.

In 2008, just a year before I joined the trading floor - the stock market had collapsed. The S&P 500 index dropped nearly 60% in a span of approximately five hundred days. Trillions of dollars evaporated, and retail traders were punished harshly. The bull party ended abruptly.

Our training program was concurrent with the last stages of the bear market. Call volumes were high and wait times were over one hour to speak with a trader. The market was in a stage of despair.

To handle the influx of calls, our training program was cut short and we were put on the phones a lot earlier than intended. My biggest challenge was operating the multiple systems that were not integrated. Each one had its own intricacies and nuances. You used one system to pull a client profile, a second to check trade status and orders and so on. Alt-tab was your best friend.

My very first call was a customer who wanted to check their buying power. Because the stocks he owned on margin had dropped so much in value, our credit department sold his stock position at a loss as he was underfunded. This meant he no longer owned the stocks he purchased and had very little cash left in his account after absorbing the loss. Markets were dropping so fast that by the time you filled out an order ticket to sell your position, the stock could have dropped another percent or two. The client on the phone hadn't been checking his account statement out of fear of the devastating results to his portfolio. He was scared, and he wasn't alone.

The next call was a client in a similar situation. How much money do I have, he asked. I explained the margin call situation again, and his response has stuck in my head until today. He said, "great that's enough for a funeral service; send it to my bank account. I'll need it soon." I got off the phone sick to my stomach, and alerted compliance of this incident. We had to report any incidents where clients were threatening us or themselves. This is the reality of a market crash to the retail trader.

Call after call the story was the same, big losses and lots of emotional pain. I felt more like a psychiatrist than a representative at a trading desk.

After just two hours on the phone taking repeated calls of agony, I took a short break and ran to the washroom. I was so sick I literally threw up. And that is how my dream career on the trading floor started. Carnage.

At this same time, I continued to trade my account and was short everything. I even tried to short Scotiabank stock. Thankfully my manager told me it was against the company policy before I pulled the trigger. Employees at the bank are not allowed to be short the company stock or own put options on it. My boss saved me a walk of shame to the compliance department, and maybe even a pink slip. This was my first lesson of the restraints on your personal trading when you sign up for this career. I was short, and the clients on the phone were long.

I constantly thought, how could this be happening? How could people be holding their position through this entire drop? Worse yet, some were even buying the dips all the way down, causing losses to escalate at an alarming rate. How didn't anyone see this avalanche coming? Everyone must have heard the overhanging snow breaking off at the top and start to tumble. Why were they waiting below helplessly? Do something, take action and try to survive!

During this same time I published a technical analysis blog. I warned everyone I could in November of 2007 that it was time to take profit and set levels to exit positions. It wasn't that I was expecting the massive crash we got, it was just a cautionary tale to take profit and reduce position sizing.

The truth is that no one knows where the market is going, and anyone who thinks they do is delusional. If anyone could know with certainty where the market is headed, it would already be there. It is not a science of prediction. Reading in real time, however, helps you see the crash as it is happening and lets you take corrective action. Traders can anticipate markets, but our profit is made in responding to them. An analyst anticipates, a trader executes. This is a difference of a salary versus a variable income opportunity with no ceiling.

All my blog posts were warnings in real time. It fell on deaf ears. The website statistics were telling me I was reaching very few people outside of my circle of friends and family. While I was prepared for a big market sell-off I was hoping it would not happen. I knew it would hurt millions of people who worked hard to save their money, but had little knowledge on the inner workings of the stock market. All they knew was to buy low and sell high, yet in an enormous bull market their brokerage accounts showed evidence they repeatedly bought high and sold low. I could see their trades in real time on the trading desk. It was shocking to see such irrational decisions being made with one's life savings.

My emotions were very complex the first few days of my new job. During the evenings I was busy writing detailed blog posts and closing profitable positions, while in the day time I was talking to clients facing financial ruin. Every day was the same roller coaster ride with the same outcome. It started as shock which eventually morphed to anger and ended in sadness. It was never ending, and it was exhausting.

And the most important part was that it ultimately led me to action. Those calls would fuel my life purpose.

In 2009 the market bottomed out and started to rebound as the $700 billion Troubled Asset Relief Program (TARP), launched by Ben Bernanke in late 2008, started to take hold in the financial system. This was the first of three rounds of quantitative easing as it was called, or more simply put, printing money out of thin air and circulating it into the banking system. The liquidity boost helped stabilize equity markets.

To this day most people don't really know what stopped the market crash dead in its tracks in 2009. In simple terms, banks took on enormous risk and when they were on the brink of failure, they were bailed out by the government using taxpayer money. You worked hard and paid tax, which went to save the banks, while your retirement portfolio took on the full losses. Then, during the recession after the banks were bailed out and survived, you likely lost your job due to market conditions. That was the raw deal. The hardest working people lost the most and bailed out the banks. Most have still not recovered to this day. Who was going to bail them out? No one. This filled me with anger, and more importantly the passion to be the change I wanted to see.

The people on the other side of the phone lost a lot of money, and some even lost everything. It was a dark time. I had to do something about it, I had to help. I knew that it was too late for this recession, but I knew that when the next one came roaring around I would be in a position to have a voice. I made a promise to myself.

In 2011, after working for two years as a customer service representative I was accepted into the trader licensing program. The training was self-study material that was required by the regulatory body in Ontario. Most of the focus was on compliance, ethics and regulation. After thirty days of shadowing other traders and studying, the last step was an interview with our director of compliance. It was the hardest interview of my life.

In the span of four hours, he went through one million questions designed to test my decision making process and awareness. When I stopped to think about the answer, he would assume the role of a client and say, "Hello? Are you still there? Hurry up, I have to take my kids to school." He was pretending to be a demanding client to test my ability to deal with a heavy workload under pressure. This was designed to prepare me for what was to come.

As a little aside here, I remember the biggest gaffe on the trading desk. One of the traders confused the dollar value of the transaction with the number of shares he was supposed to buy. To illustrate this example, instead of buying one hundred thousand dollars' worth of a certain stock, he bought one hundred thousand shares. The massive buy order that flooded the market drove the price sharply higher. Unwinding that position was a nightmare, as it was a thinly traded stock. This caused a massive loss for the business and stuck the error account with a huge debit. This is why these interviews are so intense. Awareness and accuracy is mandatory.

After three and a half hours, my interview ended a little shorter than usual. Dazed and confused I stared at him and waited for him to say something. He did the same, with a faint smile some would confuse for a smirk. After a few moments of silence he said, "You passed, well done - welcome to the trading desk."

I completed my paper work that day and a few weeks later it became official, I had achieved my goal of becoming a professional trader. I was a licensed investment dealer in all ten Canadian provinces. My internal trader identification number was S1A: Me, George Papazov. You can search the Canadian Securities Administrators website and see the record and history of my registration. Sometimes I still do it for nostalgia.

In that moment I thought back to the song with Allen, and smiled as the lyrics of "we will always make it" played in my mind. I thought of the sacrifices my parents made to leave everything they had built back home to come to Canada for a better life for us. Every struggle, challenge and difficulty in my life was made whole. It was all worth it. S1A was more than my trader code; it was a symbol of accomplishment. I took in a deep breath and savored the moment.

The two years that followed were amazing. I was trading for clients and for myself. I was going through the options licensing program and preparing for the next step of my career.

While I was a trader, I also laid the foundation for what would later become TRADEPRO Academy, by creating the Foundations Course. This was my side hustle project. Everyday after work, I went home and worked another four hours or more, to create courses and training materials that would help people navigate the next recession like pros. I had never forgotten the clients I talked with in my first few days. Next time the crash happened, I wanted people to be making money. I wanted people to have control. I kept the operation very low key as it was a gray area to run a business while being employed full time. To do this, you require permission by the compliance department.

During this time our bank bought a leading brokerage firm in Canada, and there was a massive amalgamation underway. Project Top Gun, as it was called internally. Two cultures collided, which created major career opportunities outside of the trading desk.

Once the integration project was complete, an opportunity came up to join the branch channel sales team. This was a business development role in educating and incentivizing advisors to open trading accounts for their clients. I was torn if I should switch to sales or stick with my career as a trader. To be quite frank, trading on the desk at a bank is very restrictive on how you can trade on your own account. There were rules, limitations and the constant review of your trades and statements by a compliance officer. I learned that being a professional trader meant you are trading for others, at the expense of your own opportunity. Moving to the sales side meant I could actually further my own trading career, while learning another perspective of the business.

I accepted the offer as a business development associate. I maintained my trading license as I was the only person on the sales team with a true trading background, and would occasionally be sent to the trading queue to cover overflow calls. I loved the variety to work for two business lines. Within a year, I was quickly promoted to a business development manager.

My personal trading took off, and I built new skills and networked with high level employees at the company. I enjoyed training thousands of advisors about trading and even attending meetings with high net worth clients. I was responsible for hundreds of branches across multiple provinces. This is when I discovered I had a passion for teaching others, and seeing the light bulb go on when they understood the advantages of self-directed investing. I channeled my passion and experience into my work and thrived in the role as a result.

My assigned branches were smashing targets, as the entire sales team's value and contribution to the bank grew. We were front and center and enjoyed the perks, trips, sales conferences and mostly the salary that came along with the job.

It was a very happy time in my life, and it turned out to be the highpoint of my career working for someone else.

Your career is like a party; you want to get there early to enjoy yourself and witness the progression of the night. You want to have responsibility for creating a fun atmosphere. Yet, you also want to start walking to the coat check during the peak so you can get out before the crowd.

I sensed that tides were shifting in the retail bank channel. The brokerage business was losing it's priority in the retail banking channel, as the focus shifted more to savings and deposit growth. I knew these changes would not be to our benefit. The party was nearing the peak. Our business line was booming, bonuses were growing and I found myself looking towards the coat check. There was no one in line. Was it time to walk?

Here I was again, like many times before in my life, I had a big decision to make.

This was the biggest and scariest one yet.

CHAPTER EXERCISE

The moment you decide to learn about this business, you become a trader. By reading this book, you have already assumed the identity that you are a trader. Say it to yourself now, "I am a trader."

Many people see themselves as "becoming traders," which creates thoughts of doubt in their heads. The resulting negative emotions create a reality of someone becoming a trader, someone who struggles but is not yet a trader. As long as you see yourself as becoming a trader, you will never become one. You have to decide right now that you already are a trader. Think of this, if you are going to be making consistent returns in the future, are you not the same person today who will evolve into that reality? Therefore, if you are ever going to be a successful trader then you already are one now. Say it one more time, like you believe it, "I am a trader!"

Congratulations, welcome to your new identity.

In Chapter 8 I will share some tools that you can use to develop and maintain a winning mindset. For now, the belief you are a trader now is enough to cause powerful change.

At this time I think it is important to begin practicing gratuity. In life we are constantly thinking about the past and future. However, the past is gone and the future may never come. Everything you need is here, in the now. In this moment is where all creation happens. Gratuity is all about taking a moment on a daily basis to reflect on what you are grateful for, and to appreciate what you have.

Building a gratuity journal is simple, and I will show you the steps below. All you will need is an empty notebook. You can perform this practice on a digital notebook, but I think it is most powerful when you are using good old-fashioned pen and paper.

Let's try this exercise now. Before you move to the steps below; get a piece of paper and a pen and sit in a comfortable position in a quiet environment.

Step 1: Start on a fresh page by writing the date on the top. You can do this journaling in the morning or evening, whenever you feel it is right for you. I prefer to do it in the morning as it creates an appreciation mood that helps power start my day. This is a personal preference, and I would suggest you try both to see what you like better.

Step 2: Write down one person you are grateful to have in your life. Now close your eyes and think of that person as if they were in front of you. Experience the joy of being their presence, tell them how much you are grateful for them and what makes you feel that way. Then send them a feeling of love, joy and happiness.

Step 3: Directly below, write down one physical possession you are grateful to own, which brings you joy and satisfaction. Now close your eyes and follow the same process as the step above, and for all the remaining steps.

Step 4: Now choose a nature experience to be grateful for. It could be the fresh water you drank, the gentle breeze, the birds chirping, the limitless blue sky; or anything else. Spend a few moments being thankful, and enjoying nature in your visualization.

Step 5: Lastly, you can write down anything else you are grateful for and allow your thoughts to flow freely. By this point, you have been immersed in gratuity and you may find that ideas and things are popping up on their own. Think about how grateful you are for them, thank them, and send them love, joy and happiness.

That is all it really takes to supercharge your day and experience the beauty of living in the present. Savor every moment, for it is all we have in life. You will notice that you have a lot of things and people to be grateful for. Every morning, I perform an identical gratuity journal.

I have enjoyed the benefits of this exercise tremendously, as I will tell you more about in the coming chapters.

CHAPTER 5
THE BIG DECISION

Through the years of working in the trading industry, I developed personally and professionally. I am very grateful for the people I met and the milestones I have achieved in my corporate life. I have been lucky and blessed.

Working for someone else, however, was silencing an entrepreneurial part of me that was getting restless inside. I knew that I was on a cushy path to a fruitful and safe career. On the outside I was living the dream, but on the inside my true desire and passion was being ignored.

In January of 2016, I drafted my resignation letter. As I was typing it I couldn't help but feel like I was letting down a lot of people. My parents, who sacrificed everything for me to have this opportunity. My friends, who looked up to me and respected me for my accomplishments. My boss who invested a lot of money and time in developing my talents. The company who employed me all these years and invested in my growth, and a lot of others it would take a full book to name. What would they think of this decision? Would they understand it, or would they think I was being ungrateful?

There was one person who gave me courage and strength. Her name was Reese, my girlfriend at the time. She supported me and even encouraged me to make the leap. She could see I was having an internal conflict, and sensed it before I could. At the time Reese was close to leaving her corporate career at a tech company in pursuit of running her own business also. We had been living together for the last four years. Her unconditional love and support is a big part of my story. She really is my soulmate, and a few years later I got married to the woman of my dreams.

After drafting my resignation letter, I showed it to one of my coworkers and told him I was thinking of pulling the trigger. He looked at me and told me, "you better hide that until you're ready." This wasn't the feedback I expected, but he was right. I second-guessed the timing of the decision, and that letter sat in the drawer for the next nine months.

During a branch visit, I met with a client who wanted to deposit a large sum of money. So I attended the sales meeting to support the financial advisor at the branch. The client told me his story of how he lost everything in the housing bubble collapse. This led him to a divorce, and he started a contracting business to stay busy and make his comeback in life. His story touched me deeply, and that night in my dreams I relived the phone conversations I witnessed in the beginning of my career in vivid detail. This time it felt more like my intuition giving me a signal to make a move than it did a coincidence of events. It was time to take action.

The next morning I resorted to my favorite method of decision making. I took out a piece of paper and took inventory of the pros and cons of leaving my career behind and trading full time.

My fiancé and I had built a nice life for ourselves. We owned a nice portfolio of real estate properties, worked hard after our regular work shift on our own business and it was paying off. We were putting in longer hours on our side hustles than we did at work, and that came at the cost of sleep. It felt like I was possessed, in a good way. I needed to spend all my time on building my passion, and working for myself. My trading was generating consistent income and I had enough cash flow saved for six months of expenses without having to dig into my trading account balance. The decision was easy, it was now a matter of going through the motions.

When I told Reese about this plan, her response was a simple "Okay, I'm excited for you." I could tell she really believed in me. There was no hesitation or question; she was more interested in helping me make it work than anything else. She is the most supportive person in my life. She told me she was going to resign as well and work on growing her business. And there we were, at the same point in life at the same time. Leaving a promising career is hard, but if you have a support mechanism in place it becomes less stressful. The pressure is absent, and the excitement is abundant.

In September of 2016, I walked up to my director and asked to talk to him. We walked over to a boardroom nearby, and before I could speak he asked me, "When's the date." I knew that people could tell my passion was split between my career at Scotiabank and my desire to be self-employed - but I didn't know it was that obvious. At that point in my life I can be honest and say I was half-assing two things at the same time; my business and my job. Having to live in the shadows was stressful. I felt like I was doing a good job balancing the two, but I think everyone else knew my passion started when my day job shift ended.

People know the things we try to hide. It's a function of the subconscious mind to be able to read body language and emotion. In fact, only 7% of communication is attributed to the words we use. The rest is how we say the words; body language, tonality, volume, etc.

It's only ourselves we are fooling by covering up our true passion and trying to conform to a template because we are afraid to act on our real desires. I had enough of this double life.

I handed my director the resignation letter, and we proceeded to work out how the last two weeks of my career would look. I agreed to help onboard a new team member and I left the company gracefully. In my life, my relationships have always been the most important thing to me. I think it's important to create win-win scenarios and to treat others with respect. To this day my former director and I are good friends, and meet for dinner and bounce ideas back and forth regularly. I was truly lucky to have a great boss like him, and I'm very grateful for the leadership qualities he taught me by embodying them himself. He led by example, and I practice the same style of leadership to this day myself.

On Friday September 16th, 2016 at 4PM EST I left work for the final time, leaving behind a six figure salary and a promising career at one of Canada's biggest banks.

My corporate career ended, and my journey to success and freedom had just started.

In the first few months of trading full time, things were very challenging. I was losing money more days than I was winning. The winning days were small, and the losing days were large. I wasn't really concerned, because I knew the transition period would take some time. This was all about acclimatizing to the new level of my career than it was about reaching the peak of the mountain as quickly as possible. In order to preserve my capital, I scaled down my trading to help me scale up my confidence. When you're in a rut, it's always better to trade smaller to work your way out than it is to double your size and increase your risk. I learned in my career that you scale up with confidence and success, you reward your positive behaviors by giving yourself bigger opportunities. This lesson alone is enough to turn around your performance.

While focusing most of my attention on my trading, I was operating my business, TRADEPRO Academy. In 2014 I started a weekly webinar that helped traders prepare for the upcoming week. It includes analysis, levels and trade ideas. When I first started this weekly webinar, I was speaking every Sunday at 8PM EST to just six people. One week it exceeded ten participants for the first time, and I was so happy. If I only helped ten people achieve their goals and live a life of financial independence, then it was damn well worth it.

In 2016, after I left my job, I was doing this same webinar for just over fifteen people. My business was more of a hobby than a business. It was an insignificant income, but a very rewarding feeling of teaching others. What was most important was the community, and having a place to socialize with other like-minded people I valued most. I'll touch more on this in a later chapter.

After a few weeks of struggling, I finally stabilized and was consistently making a daily income that matched my corporate income. This gave me confidence, and helped me settle into my routine. I was doing very well while I was working, but to hit consistency when everything was on the line felt like a giant weight was lifted off my shoulders. It validated my decision to leave a stable job and work for a variable income.

For those that know me, they know me as a very social person. I was trading from my downtown loft apartment on the second floor. My commute to the office was a total of twelve steps, from my bed to the trading desk. It was great for the first year, and then it became lonely. The successes and challenges felt...insignificant. It felt like a tree-falling-in-the-forest-and-no-one-could-hear-it type of thing. Did it happen? Did all the success in the world for me matter if I couldn't share my true gift with others? I wanted a more social setting; a place where I can cause change and work on a team.

So I decided to open a daily trading room and create an online meeting environment for other traders looking to connect and trade together. Who said this had to be an individual game, why couldn't it be a team sport?

At first I was nervous to trade live and operate a trading room. I felt like the pressure of speaking about trading while doing it in real time would be immense. I felt like I would be half-assing it again. Thankfully, I was wrong. In fact, from the very first day in the trading room it was a big hit. My trading continued to improve, and the room popularity grew. As the room grew, the ability to talk with others and learn from them in a collaborative setting helped my personal trading propel forward even more. This in turn brought more attention to the room, and so the cycle repeated.

One day that year, we surpassed thirty members in the room and I almost cried. My passion was becoming reality. The atmosphere was full of energy and it was thrilling to tackle the markets and win together.

Since I started my career on the brokerage trading floor, all I wanted was to trade my capital with a group of people to whom I could relate. I went to school for four years and worked at a professional trading company for five. I did not find the feeling I was after. For the first time, I really felt like I belonged and I knew this was the start of something bigger than me. I felt an electrifying energy while I ran the room, and I channeled higher power and intuition to guide me. I felt like I was doing the right thing with my life. I found my purpose.

To this day, when people succeed in this business and share their stories with me I get goosebumps and a blissful joy fills my heart to the brim.

In the meantime, my wife was working beside me on her own business. Since both leaving our corporate jobs in the same month a year ago, we spent our entire days together. Spending time with her is my favorite hobby on this planet, so I was very fulfilled.

If you know me, you know I can get excited and loud. I am a very passionate person. I was getting too excited and too loud too often, and distracted Reese very frequently. She is the type to get into deep flow and stay there for hours, whereas I can barely sit still for thirty consecutive minutes.

I laughed, I screamed out of joy and mostly I was slowly going crazy in my home office. It was one full year since I left my corporate job and things were amazing. In reflection, at that time the only regret I had about leaving was not doing it sooner.

I loved how rewarding it was to teach others to trade, and also to trade with them in real time. In 2017, I had found my true calling, and that was to run TRADEPRO Academy and help people change their lives.

No one cares about your money more than you do, so why let anyone else manage what you worked so hard to create? Who is better at caring for your family than yourself?

It was time for traders to have a community that reflected the reality of learning to trade. It is really hard when it's done the wrong way, but it is possible when you belong to a winning team that genuinely cares about you and your progress. I wanted to create an environment that was educational, fun and raw. This was my calling; this was truly something that was bigger than me and the reason I was put on the earth. The industry was all about selling you overnight success, and my mission was to disrupt the space and create the world's best online trading community.

But I couldn't do this from my bedroom, so I decided it was time for me to get an office.

CHAPTER EXERCISE

The decision for me to leave a secure career was not easy, but it was necessary to achieve my goals. Just like I had to decide to grow my business, in your trading career you will eventually be faced with the decision of scaling up your strategy. At some point you will want to go bigger, it's a part of the natural progression of a trader.

How does one do this? When is the right time?

I will include a copy of the TRADEPRO Academy scaling plan for futures traders at the end of this exercise, but first let's dig into some key considerations.

The most important thing is to realize that you want to increase your trading size in direct proportion to your experience level and the success you are already having.

If you are still working towards becoming profitable consistently, the answer is you should not be scaling up. There are no definitively right times, but there are wrong times. This is one of them. If you do not have the experience and mental mindset to stop losing, scaling up will only cause you to lose more money faster. If you are in this situation, your money--and more importantly your time--are better invested in improving your trading psychology and getting more screen time. These two things will yield much better returns on your investment with very little risk, in comparison to adding size to a losing state. When in doubt, always start with psychology and more screen time - this is the holy grail you were looking for.

Now, if you're a trader who's hitting consistency and seeing success with their strategy, when should you scale up?

The answer is not simple, and it varies according to each person and their behavior traits, motivators and subconscious mind programming.

Here are some considerations when designing your scaling up strategy:

Scale up with market money. This means only trade bigger when you have accumulated market profits in excess to your starting capital. This cushion gives you profits to risk on a larger trade size, that way you don't leverage up your savings but rather the profits already generated by them.

Scale down on fifty loss. When you increase your size, you have to identity and cap your risk. The concept here is to only lose half, or fifty percent of the profits you made trading with smaller size.

I think it's important to illustrate with an example at this point.

Let's assume you deposited $10,000 into your trading account as starting capital. After successfully growing your account to $17,000 you decide it's time to increase your trading size. This increases your trading risk per trade as well. Your total market profit is $7,000. Half of that is $3,500. Once you scale up, you only have $3,500 of risk capital or you drop back down to your previous size. This helps you scale on market profits and with success.

In addition to these simple rules, you also want to consider your psychological limit.

Every person has developed their winning mindset to a different degree. You have to understand that without constantly working to expand your growth mindset, your scaling efforts will eventually hit a ceiling. You will hit a profit target that surpasses your money mindset level. This is when it gets fun, as it now becomes all about developing yourself to break through prior plateaus. We have an entire psychology course designed with personal growth in mind. It would be hard to give you personalized and useful coaching through a book.

I can however give you some questions to get you thinking about scaling up like a professional.

If you were a person applying to trade your capital, what is the maximum size you would approve?

What is the minimum size you would require?

What is the last thing you can remember that you have done with complete confidence?

How long did you perform this thing before you became confident?

How will you know when you are this confident with your trading?

When will you develop a complete and comprehensive scaling plan?

What resources do you already have to create this plan?

What resources will you need?

Here is a copy of the TRADEPRO Academy Futures Scaling Plan, as promised.

The lot size at the top shows how many futures contracts are traded. The dollar amount below it is the daily profit goal you are striving for. Directly below that is the number of months to hit this daily target before you scale up, but you have to generate the target profit also. If you lose a percentage of the surplus profit below, or the dollar value below that, you move back in the grid to the previous position. If you are trading just a single lot at that point, it's time to go back to testing and development of your strategy.

So as an example, to move from two lots to three, you will need to:

- Make $250 US a day for 2 months consecutively

- And make at least $10,000 in total profit in the two months

- You advance to three lots and increase your scale

If you are trading two lots you will drop back to one when:

- You lose 75% of the profits you generated with a single lot

- If you lose $2,250 USD in total you move back in the grid

- You are now trading one lot

This system is not perfect for every trader, or any trader. It is specific to futures trading using our order flow strategies. The intent of a scaling plan is to keep you on pace for constant growth, and to limit the risk exposure you are taking on to achieve this same growth. There is a misconception in our business that we are trading for profit. The money is the reward for managing risk. What matters is risk-adjusted profit. One of my favorite sayings is that profit is the reward of being a disciplined risk manager.

The grid is an illustration, and is not suggested for use out of the box. However, you do want to have a scaling plan before you start trading bigger. Creating a plan is not optionable, it is necessary for your long term success.

GEORGE PAPAZOV

CHAPTER 6
GROWING TO GIVING

O n Monday January 1st of 2018, I moved into the upstairs floor of a two story commercial loft near my residence. It sounds fancy, but it was literally a bedroom on the residential floor of the property. Basically, I moved from my bedroom to someone else's. The space was very small, and also very bright with panoramic views of Lake Ontario. Of all the things that it was, my favorite was that it was affordable and the lease term was only twelve months. This provided a lot of flexibility for future growth.

I worked there myself for the first few months, and have very fond memories of the humble beginnings of TRADEPRO Academy. During the mornings I hosted the trading room, and in the afternoons I created as much content as possible. YouTube videos, emails, blog posts, workbooks and online course videos. On most nights, I left very late in the evenings and occasionally even in the early hours of the next day. I liked to tell people that I lived in the office and visited my home for a quick nap. All that mattered to me was that our trading community was progressing, and many new members were learning how to reach consistent profitability in the early stages of their trading career. The success of our community motivated me to work fourteen hour days, with optimism and a smile on my face through every minute. I was very grateful for the opportunity to live my dream life.

Trading and running the business kept me extremely busy through the cold winter months. After the first quarter of 2018, it became obvious that I needed help. The workload continued to increase, and I needed to hire someone who cared about our community and the business as much as I did. I was lucky to find some amazing and passionate people, which I will tell you about a little later in this chapter.

I had a massive vision for what I wanted TRADEPRO Academy to become. Reality was quickly catching up to the vision and I was preparing for a big expansion in the upcoming year.

When I first moved to the neighborhood where we currently live with my wife, I always loved the look of one of the office buildings in particular. We live in a mixed residential and commercial area. This building was beautiful, it fascinated me and it spoke to me from the day I saw it five years before. From 1899 to 1950 it was a carpet factory in a very industrial part of the city. Now it was a renovated commercial loft building with nineteen foot ceilings, exposed brick and modern luxurious finishes. The exterior was also brick and beautiful vines ran the height of the structure. It was perfect. Best of all it was in the same neighborhood as my apartment. I dreamed of working in that building for years.

In November of 2018 I began searching for our next office. I spent three hours combing through office lease websites, online directories and Google searches. Toronto is a hot commercial real estate market, though, and very few properties matched the environment I was envisioning.

The next day I went online to continue the search for the next TRADEPRO Academy headquarters. The first search was a beautiful space that was available in February of 2019, just twelve weeks away. I was shocked when I clicked the link and found out that it was the very same building I described above. It was like it was meant to be. There was a lot of demand and I had to act quickly if I was to have any chance at all of leasing it. I called the landlord right away, and went to see it the same day in the afternoon. I filled out an application and submitted my offer. A few days later it was accepted, and we officially found our new headquarters. It really was a powerful coincidence that felt more like fate. Five years after seeing the space I loved, we were moving into it. Not something like it, but the exact building. The universe really does work miracles.

On a cold February Friday, after we finished trading in our daily room, we started packing. We worked in a tiny room that didn't require a lot of packing. There were three of us working in a bedroom sized space. It literally was a bedroom on the residential floor of a commercial space I had rented for myself. I really did not foresee the business growing so quickly that it would need to house three people within the year. By the evening, we had moved everything to the new office and setup the computers and internet. We were wired and fired up for the upcoming Monday. This was a new start.

The team had grown very quickly in just one year. Victorio was our first full time hire, who I met through a very funny incident I just have to share with you.

While I was working at the bank, I remember going to a Starbucks at lunch to check on the markets and put in some limit orders. I bumped into one of the patrons as I was putting milk in my coffee. He walked over to my table where I was sitting a few minutes later and asked me what I was doing. I explained what I do and we exchanged numbers. He was also Bulgarian and we had a lot in common. Over the coming months, we talked about a lot of business opportunities and the markets in general. One day he called me and asked me if I could speak to his son, who just dropped out of school and needed some career advice.

A few weeks later we schedule a meeting at a Starbucks in between where we both lived. I walked into the door and saw him sitting with his son. The kid had a black eye and a blank expression. That was Victorio. Over the years he has grown and matured into a very impressive young man. He had a heart of passion and a desire to succeed on his own terms, and he really flourished when he was introduced to trading. To this day, Victorio has a massive influence on the business and can be heard daily in our trading room. When I look back at these events, I smile and remind myself that you never know who you're going to bump into and the ripple effect it could have on your life. Every time I'm at Starbucks I have a good chuckle, especially when I go with Victorio.

Our second full time employee was Mark, who joined us a few months prior to our move. I met Mark while I worked at Scotiabank on a routine visit to a branch. While I was visiting branches, a common reaction was a lack of care for investments. Most retail branch employees just want to sell you a deposit product or credit card. Mark was different; he loved investments and we sat in his office talking for hours. I left his office after exchanging business cards knowing that our paths will cross again at some point. A year later he joined the brokerage I worked for, and he sat on the currency desk. In the summer of 2018 he left the corporate world and joined our team. He creates amazing content and is a regular presence in our YouTube videos and writes the weekly currency report.

The third and most recent hire was Azalia, who I first met at the brokerage as well. My first encounter with her was when she came over to shadow with the sales team for a day. I remember her asking great questions and really being able to connect with me in a short period of time. Very few people have this innate ability to create such genuine and strong relationships so quickly. She genuinely cares about people and asks amazing questions. Azalia was a gift to the team and rounded out our skillset very nicely. Today she helps us provide excellent service and experience to our community. She's a strong person and does a lot of heavy lifting on a daily basis behind the scenes.

When you see us working in the office, you would think we are one big family just having fun. And it's true, our entire community is a giant family. When we immigrated to Canada, I lost connection to my cousins, grandparents and friends. I had a sister, mom and dad and nearly five thousand miles of distance between the rest of the relatives I grew up with in my early years. In short, I got the big family I've always wanted.

The team was the kind of team that I dreamed of working with. And that's how we became the dream team. This is what we call each other in meetings and company wide emails.

In 2017, when I still ran the trading room by myself from my bedroom, I had a few text chats with a new member who was very engaged. He was full of knowledge and had some great insight into the oil market. One day I asked him if he would like to jump on the mic so we can exchange some analysis. To my surprise he agreed, and I opened up his mic. He never got off the mic. He has been hosting the daily trading room with me every day since then, minus a few vacation days when he sets off in the North Georgia mountains. Stephen is one of the best oil traders I will ever know, and has become a dear friend for whom I am grateful to know. Today he runs our oil desk, and is the crude oil whisperer. He is also the patient individual helping with the editing of my first ever book-; God bless his heart for dealing with me on this project.

One last, but not least member I want to talk about is David, who I also met sometime in 2017. At the time I was interacting directly with most new members to welcome them to our community. On our first call, David told me he would be one of our most successful members, and shared his ambitious plan to make one hundred thousand dollars by the end of the year. I believed him, he had the type of drive, determination and passion you could hear in someone's voice and would not dare doubt.

David lived up to his promise, and turned a small $700 US trading account into a balance that was short of what he promised, but not by much as far as I know. It was a remarkable growth achieved by a strict focus on risk management. He worked hard, stayed humble and became super successful. He now hosts the trading room during the London hours. I never told him this, but he inspired me to continue pushing the boundaries and to make this community way larger than I had planned. He really showed me the magnitude of what was possible and it gave me the confidence to believe in myself and what we were creating. David proved to everyone that we had something special, and that he himself was a star. I started to truly believe that I could change the entire world through TRADEPRO Academy.

Getting to work with such a high performing team is humbling. I wake up every morning excited to spend my day around them. Even the days that I leave the office at midnight after a sixteen hour day, I feel energized and eager to get back at it the next morning. If I didn't live three quarters of a mile from my office, I would probably have an inflatable mattress in the corner of the trading floor.

Everything was going so amazing by the summer of 2019 that my fulfillment reached the most inner depths of my soul. I was happy. So happy that some days I held tears back when I reflected on my journey. From sleeping on the benches at an airport terminal to becoming an entrepreneur in the industry I loved. What a blessing. I reached the financial success I had longed for. I became a millionaire in my early thirties like I planned. I got to drive my dream woman in my dream car. I worked with the dream team. It was bliss.

But life is not designed for long moments of comfort and stillness. Anything that is alive is destined for growth. Growth happens in the soil of constant action. And anything that grows needs to be constantly on the outer edge of its comfort zone. If you're safe, you're playing too small.

In March of 2019 a musician I was inspired by passed away tragically due to gun violence. It saddened me, and touched me deeply. I did not know him personally, but he was so inspirational I felt like we were acquainted and united by a common vision. His music is raw and not for everyone, but the change he created was legendary. I resonated with Ermias Joseph Asghedom, known by his "Nipsey Hussle" stage name. He was someone who reached success and tried to bring back the opportunities to his community. Ermias gave hope to a neighborhood drenched in economic lack. He used the money he made from music to buy the strip mall in the neighborhood where he grew up, and provided employment opportunities to the youth. He was also involved in teaching young kids about entrepreneurship and technology innovation. The irony was that he died in front of what he built, in front of the store he owned in the same area he grew up his entire life. What a tragedy. The day he passed away, all of California felt the pain.

This event stayed on the top of mind for long enough that I interpreted it as a message from my intuition that it was time to start giving back. I remembered about Allen, and the trying times of growing up in Scarborough. From day one, my plan was to create and build wealth so I can give back. I was now in a good position to start giving back. I wanted to create change.

I asked myself, what is the right thing to do? Does one bring resources back to the neighborhood they grew up in and help those in need now, or does one create massive financial success and hope it trickles down to them eventually? What would have the most impact? What was the most sustainable action plan? Was it time to start the charity studio in honor of Allen?

It has always been my life long mission to create lasting change. I like to solve problems and to help others. Money is a tool for creation for me, it is meant to be circulated and given back. This is a concept you will never read in a finance textbook, where it's all about maximizing your personal gain. But this state of mind creates lack, and goes against a universal law. The more you give, the more you receive. And the fastest way to get something is to give it first. Giving is living.

So in the late summer of 2019 we embarked on a project to teach financial literacy to youth in troubled neighborhoods. One day after the market closed, I walked over to the whiteboard in our meeting room and wrote "financial literacy for youth" at the top. As soon as the marker made the first contact with the board, the ideas started flowing out. I came into contact with a higher power, a collective consciousness. It was electric, and it felt right. This was my sign of reassurance; this was meant to happen.

Through me, the universe created a powerful three week workshop. In the first week, we taught the concept of creating a budget and saving money early and regularly. In week two, they learned about the importance of credit, how to build it the right way and how to avoid the common pitfalls. And finally, in week three, we concluded the workshop by speaking about investing in the stock market, real estate and how to create a business by starting small.

We partnered up with a high school community center in a low income neighborhood in Toronto. At this age, kids transition to early adulthood and start to have some really complex thoughts and conflicting narratives. I wanted to share the message with them that I was in their seat at one point. I was an immigrant, and my parents came to Canada with next to nothing. I wanted them to feel inspired, moved to action and mostly loved. To know that they were perfect, capable and that they could do anything they wanted in life. The message got across, and I could see the light bulbs lighting up as the workshop progressed. They learned a lot, and I learned that today's generation of youth are extremely smart and aware. I also learned that I loved this work, and I needed to do more.

I saw their hunger for knowledge and desire for success and safety for themselves and their families. This was one of my greatest accomplishments of the year, and it has set in motion an initiative we call TRADEPRO Gives. We are on a mission to educate and create opportunities for the youth, who are the future of this planet. Since then we have sponsored local hockey teams, ran nutrition programs in multiple countries and have big plans to make a massive and sustainable impact in the coming year.

Giving back has really closed the loop on the journey that is my life. If I do nothing more than continue to build our trading community and give back to causes that will make a change for the better, I can say I've lived my life to the fullest. I feel like I have reached the pinnacle, and I also know that my intuition will continue to lead me to where it is I need to go. I'm not finished, I feel there is still a long road ahead. My intuition tells me there are big triumphs still awaiting.

But this connection to the youth got me thinking about something else, another big future milestone of my life.

My wife and I have been talking about starting our family recently.

A lot of friends and family have asked me why I have waited for so long and warned me, that chasing kids around in my forties would be exhausting. I better hurry up they tell us. But, the truth is I've been sprinting towards my dreams my entire life, what's another few years of running circles in the living room? I know that when the time is right, I will receive the energy I need.

My wife and I have come from little means to where we are today, and we have always felt like we weren't ready financially to support another person. We have both matured greatly through our entrepreneurship. I think what has made us successful, by our own right, is that we remember what it was like to have nothing but passion and dreams. For me, I want to be financially prepared before I take on the responsibility of caring for life. We have worked so hard in the last ten years, I suppose we never stopped for long enough to ask if we have achieved the level of safety we need to start a family. I'm going to be honest, I'm scared of being a father, but the fear is overwhelmed by excitement.

Besides, there is never a perfect time for anything, just a time. And that time seems to be getting closer. Being ready is an illusion, a mirage of sorts.

I'm ready for new challenges and to continue to grow.

So the plan for the future is to expand our TRADEPRO family, to help develop new successful traders who accomplish their dreams and live a life they do not need a vacation from.

In the coming year we have massive plans to create and to give back. We are only getting started.

The best part is that I no longer feel like I'm chasing wild dreams alone, I am part of a movement that is far bigger than me. This energizes me to think bigger and continue stepping out of my comfort zone, the way I have my entire life.

From my greatest wins to my biggest failures in life, the struggles to the euphoria, I'm grateful for it all.

In her 1989 hit, Cher sang "If I Could Turn Back Time."

Well, if I could, I would do it all over again; every single moment.

Your life is beautiful, cherish every moment while it lasts.

Yet, life is also short, so live it to the absolute fullest.

Give, live and repeat.

CHAPTER EXERCISE

Giving is an important part of my life. Much of today's society focuses on consuming more and paying the least amount possible. Economists might call this "maximizing personal gain." This constant goal of maximizing our personal value has created a lot of isolation and unhappiness in our generation. We often forget that we are actually a smaller part of a greater whole. Scientifically we are all interconnected, and are actually more like a single cell within an organism, as opposed to a separate organism ourselves.

As you grow personally and reach continuously higher career milestones, it's important to give back. No matter where you are today, how close or far from your ultimate goals, you have something to give. Your time, your love and your attention. Give freely and you will receive abundance.

So let's take a moment now to consider what you could give back, taking a top down approach.

- What do you want your legacy to be?
- What has helped you the most in your life?
- What is the most important thing that would need to happen to make this world a better place?
- What resources do you have?
- What is something you can start to give right now, no matter how small it may seem to you?
- How will you accomplish this giving, and when will you start?

These types of questions can help you identify an important cause.

For me it is all about financial literacy for youth. In my neighborhood, very few kids knew how to make their money work for them. They all knew they had to work for money, and what exactly they would spend it on. Investing was like a myth that everyone has heard about, but no one knew anyone who was doing it. Until my dad introduced me to trading, I was in the same boat.

My philosophy on money is that part of it gets invested in creating a better life for yourself and your family. The rest is invested into the community and deployed to make the world a better place for future generations.

Imagine how the world would look if everyone was financially literate? Imagine the innovations and advancements these young bright minds would create if they could guarantee themselves safety.

Imagine how you would benefit?

The convenience and liberties we enjoy today are on the back of the work of generations in the past. What are you doing today to move humankind forward? This in my view is the meaning of life. To learn, to use the resources you have and to create.

I encourage you to pick something you are passionate about and make a plan on how you will give back. By putting this intention in the universe, you will receive an abundance of everything you need to make it happen. Your attention plus intention manifests into reality.

When you have a purpose, when you have a cause - you have something to move towards. When you do not, you lack the magnetism to attract your dream life.

When you are motivated to move away from what you do not want, you will only move far enough to get to comfort at best. But comfort is not true happiness; it falls short of your real goals. I challenge you to think about what you do want instead, because only then do you give yourself the power to make change and achieve outcomes.

CHAPTER 7
CULTIVATING AND MAINTAINING A SUCCESS MINDSET

S uccess is all about your mindset. Nothing about it is accidental; it is entirely intentional. The good news is that there is a formula, a measured approach. The great news is that I will share this formula with you in this chapter. It changed my life.

But first, let's look at what mindset means.

I like to use the analogy of a thermostat, an idea my wife shared with me that has stuck. If the temperature in the room is at twenty degrees Celsius, and you want to turn it up to twenty eight, what do you do? You turn the thermostat to twenty eight and leave it alone. It's designed to be that simple. Then gradually the temperature will increase to the desired level over time. When it reaches twenty eight degrees, it will have achieved the goal temperature and the heating stops. While the heat is blasting and the temperature is increasing, you aren't questioning if it will happen or not, you are assuming and trusting in the final outcome. You know it's happening.

Mindset is like a thermostat, you have to set it to what you want and be patient as you move towards that goal. If you keep changing what you want, you will never get to where you want to be. Success takes time. In a society of instant gratification, we have forgotten that patience is a virtue. If we want something, we want it right now.

Unfortunately, thermostats are not designed to operate that way, and neither is your brain.

One of the biggest challenges to achieving success is that we tend to focus on things we do not want. What would happen if we did not want to be cold, but decided to do nothing about it? We remain cold, and thinking about how cold it is. If the heating system is broken, we can blame it on that. Or maybe the weather is more harsh than usual, so we blame the weather. Fact is, we can blame it on anything we like, and it doesn't change the fact that we are feeling cold. In due time, if we blame everything we can and continue to experience the problem, we will create a victim mindset for ourselves. Read carefully, as the next few sentences can change your entire life.

Thinking about something creates more of the same thing.

This brings us to the formula for achieving a success mindset and unlimited abundance in life.

In order to become successful you have to live at cause in your life, rather than in effect.

The mathematical expression is: C > E.

Living at cause means you are accepting responsibility for everything you have in your life today, good and bad. Living in effect means your life is a mere effect of other factors which you often believe to have no control over.

Let's illustrate this with an example.

Imagine purchasing shares of a stock company that you love. This company, let's call it Cause Coffee, makes your favorite caffeinated beverages. You invest $5,000 US because you think it's going to be worth way more in a few years. But it turns out that you were wrong, and instead the company goes bankrupt - losing your entire $5,000 investment. The entire decline started when it was revealed that Cause Coffee was using shady accounting practices and the company never made a penny of profit. It was all a scam from day one. Doh!

How would you feel if this actually had just happened to you?

If you are living in effect, you are extremely upset at the company's accounting team. It's not your fault, the company screwed you. How could they? It's the CEO's fault for not uncovering the scandal earlier, or the media's fault for not doing their job and investigating them. Or maybe it was the regulators fault, where the heck was the regulator? While this thinking removes the responsibility from you, it also removes your power.

You are living in the effect of someone else's cause. You learn nothing, and walk away with the impression that investing is gambling, it's a crooked marketplace. You take this attitude with you through life and decline any investment opportunity, missing all the growth potential.

Is there a different way?

If you are living at cause and this happened to you, you would start by asking yourself, "how am I at cause for this?" Then you consider that maybe you need to do more research next time before making a stock purchase. Or you learn to diversify your investments so that any one company won't have a detrimental result on your overall portfolio. Or you learn that you have a lot more learning to do before making another investment. The point is, you're learning.

After a few years of learning and living at cause, you make better investments and accumulate an abundance of wealth in your life. Then you hear someone in effect call you lucky. What do you say? What I am, is at cause!

Living at cause makes you responsible for the way your life is right now, and gives you the power to easily change it. Living at cause is so freeing and empowering, I invite you to try it for yourself.

One of my favorite question to ask people when they demonstrate they are living in effect is to ask, "How are you at cause for that?"

This is a very difficult question for someone who believes to be in effect. In fact, they may even get defensive. But when you live at cause, you know that the answer to this question will actually help them change. What benefit has a pity party ever yielded?

Going back to our previous analogy of the setting the temperature; living at cause is how you turn the mindset thermostat.

The best part is that living at cause is a simple decision, which you can choose to have made right now.

Take your power back, start experiencing the power of dream creation by living at cause.

Now that you've completed the first and most important step, let's talk about how to cultivate a winning mindset.

You will soon have the master key to open the lock of any door you want. Metaphorically speaking, of course.

The second step is to think positive thoughts only.

Negativity does not serve you, it suppresses your superpowers of manifestation. In almost any circumstances, you can reframe a negative thought into a positive one and immediately feel amazing.

Let's try a few together:

I am not good enough. > How can I improve?

I can't do it. > How can I do it?

I'm not as lucky as other people. > How can I learn to think like the lucky people?

I am not smart enough. > What can I learn to achieve my goals?

I can literally do this for hours, with any sentence that is framed in negative tense. In fact I have done it for years. I personally started with a lot of lacking beliefs myself, but I have always been a natural optimist and tend to think positively. Where I grew up, most people around me lived in effect, and sadly still do to this day. Some people's fear is losing everything they enjoy and love. But when you don't have a lot of things, you end up doing a lot of daydreaming; which naturally helps you stay in a positive mindset.

The bottom line is this: Whether you are positive or negative, it is your choice.

As you read through the above statements, did you experience the physical shift in yourself? Read them again, and be aware of your body language, mood and emotions. As you read the first part of each line, you likely slouched your shoulders forward, frowned and felt a vacuum of energy. But when we flipped those statements to positive ones, you may have smiled and even felt a surge of warming sensation.

So how often should you be thinking positive thoughts?

Always, ideally. But realistically at the beginning you want to focus on just thinking more positively as each day passes. Progress, like the thermostat takes time. Accept yourself and that this is a journey, and enjoy it.

What is most important is not to fight back against your negative thoughts. The key is to quickly acknowledge and silence them. When you find yourself thinking negatively, visualize a volume knob in your minds' eye, and as you turn it quickly, just hear the thought fade. That's right.

What happens when you silence the negative thoughts in your mind?

You are left with only the positive ones, and you are creating some amazing things that may even surprise you. You are capable of a lot more than you think, the only roadblock is ourselves.

The bottom line is that what you think in your mind will be created into reality. Everything that exists here, in the now, started with a thought. Your car, your job, your children. Buildings, bridges, bicycles and everything else, all started with a thought.

What you think is what you will create. Thoughts are commands to the unconscious mind to start the process of creation, and this is a law of the universe.

One of my favorite quotes of all time is by James Allen, who once said, "A person's mind may be likened to a garden which may be intelligently cultivated or allowed to run wild; but whether cultivated or neglected, it must, and will, bring forth."

Wow, go back and read that once more.

What you plant will grow, so plant the seed of positivity and watch it grow into a tree of opportunity.

Now that you are living at cause and intentionally thinking only thoughts that serve you, big changes are on the horizon. And remember, you must constantly work on improving yourself and maintaining a positive mindset.

Just like a high performance car needs more regular service and higher quality lubricants, so does your mind.

One of the ways to stay on top of your personal development goes in line with the previous chapter. Find a community that keeps you stay accountable for living at cause, and a place where a positive mindset is a standard.

Also I will also share a nine-day action plan to help you shift your mind to positive thinking at the end of this chapter, in addition to a list of my all-time favorite books on this subject.

Lastly, I want to leave you with a fascinating study to illustrate the importance of a positive mindset on your life.

The University of Pennsylvania conducted a study over twenty two years with three hundred and fifty thousand people. To say this study was massive is an understatement. Researchers would call the participants every week at random times of the day and asked them a series of questions.

One of the questions was "What are you thinking about right now"?

When they analyzed the data they found a remarkable difference in the answers of the top ten percent of the most successful people, versus the bottom ninety percent.

The top ten percent of people answered that they thought about what they want and how to get those things. They thought about goals, priorities, actions and activities they would do to move towards their goals and desires. They thought about solutions.

And the bottom ninety percent? They often answered that they thought about what they didn't want, and who was to blame for their problems. They spent their time living in effect, and likely felt powerless to make changes in their lives. What a sad way to choose to live.

We all have a garden with perfect soil, ready to grow whatever you are willing to plant.

What have you been planting?

What will you be planting now instead?

Whatever it is, it will be sure to grow.

CHAPTER EXERCISE

In this chapter exercise I will provide you a nine day challenge that I crafted, which will help you shift to a positive mindset. It is very important to complete this challenge in nine consecutive days. It only takes a few minutes of your day. The return on this investment of your time, may be larger than any return on any investment you will ever make. It was for me.

So commit to taking the challenge and start right now.

Day One:

Get a piece of paper and write the date on the top. Split the page vertically into two columns, on top of the first column, write the word "Positive". On the second column, write the word "-VE". This reads as negative, without the need to constantly see this word and constantly plant it into your subconscious.

Your goal on the first day is to simply become aware of your thoughts. Notice what thoughts are popping up naturally. What are they about, and how often do they occur? What are the recurring themes of the positive ones, and what about the negative?

All you have to record on this day is the tally, how many are positive and how many are negative? Now take the total of positive thoughts and divide it by the total sum of the positive and negative to get a percentage.

Example, if you had 10 positive thoughts and 60 negative, you would divide 10 into 70 for a total of 14 percent. At this point this number means nothing, it is only a reference. Keep this page somewhere, you will need it on day nine. That's it for day one, congratulations.

Days Two to Eight:

For a full week, every time you notice a negative thought imagine turning down a volume knob quickly and hear the sound of the thought fading to complete silence. Do this every single time you receive a negative thought. Remember, you are not trying to avoid negative thoughts or even oppose them. You are also not fighting them or judging them, you are simply accepting the message and silencing it with the volume knob in your mind's eye.

You may begin to even enjoy this process, as it is liberating to free your mind from the constant barrage of negative thoughts and voices. You will be having fun at this point, while your physiology will be changing as you progress through the week. You are making powerful changes at the subconscious level, that will also be apparent to the conscious level. You may even receive comments like, "Wow, you're so positive lately". Keep up the good work.

Day Nine:

Get out the same piece of paper from day one.

Flip it over and write the date at the top, and the same two columns as you did on day one. As you go about your day, you will be fully aware of most of your thoughts. You have been practicing this for a week, and are now a natural. Each time they surface, silence them if they are negative.

Record how many of the thoughts are negative and positive on the columns. At night, as you settle down and get ready for bed tally the totals. Once again, divide the positive thoughts into the total of all thoughts recorded.

Now, compare your percentage from day one to day nine. What are the results? You will see a significant improvement, it may even shock you. Awesome work, you are changing your life.

Days Ten to ∞ (infinity)

Now continue the process from days two to eight for the rest of your life. At some point you will have no thoughts to turn down, as you will be a well-oiled positivity machine firing on all cylinders. By this point, your life has changed significantly, and you are even a whole new person. You can continue to record and track your thoughts if you wish, but you will soon be seeing the results in the creation that is occurring in all areas of your life.

I have been doing this since I left my corporate job to work for myself, and have discovered some of my most successful business ideas during this period. I am happy to report that I am exceptionally positive at all times, to the annoyance of some. I am not going to say I never have negative thoughts, but if I do I no longer notice them as they are automatically silenced on the first syllable.

As you continue to practice positivity on a daily basis, you too will be cultivating a success mindset. You will be planting the seeds of positivity in the garden of growth.

Bonus: A Word on Intuition

When you are thinking positively often and are focusing on what you want, you align all your attention to your intentions. As this process automates in your subconscious it begins changing your identity, you are becoming a successful person. One of "the lucky few."

Now that you have silenced the thoughts which do not serve you, you will experience a big increase in thoughts that serve you. You will get messages at random times that seem like good ideas that come from outside your mind. This is called intuition, and it is a miracle.

Intuition is like an antenna.

As you start sending out positive signals into the universe, you will start to receive messages. These will be in the form of suggestions, ideas and possible actions. You are receiving solutions! Your antenna is now tuned. No matter how weird or random they may seem to you; these signals are guidance to take you to the target you have programmed into your subconscious through your thought commands.

I always listen to my intuition, even if my logical mind is confused and unsure how doing these intuitive actions will get me to my goal. Intuition will lead you through the path of least resistance to your target, by universal law.

Follow your intuition - it is the miracle of life, and the tether line to collective consciousness.

Lastly, when you receive intuition; you must take action quickly. When you have an idea and your intuition sends you a message on the next step, if you choose not to receive it someone else will. Once you put an idea into the universe, it must be created.

Have you ever experience a situation where you have an idea for something new, and after hesitating for weeks you see that invention come out exactly as you thought of it? You say to your friends, "that was my idea, crazy." You are right that it was your idea, but if you don't act someone else will receive the message of creation. When the phone rings, pick it up and take the call.

Intuition is a form of channeling source energy. A lot of what I create in my business and life is accomplished through this method. The more you develop your intuitive muscle the stronger the connection becomes.

Call it what you will, but make sure you call it because it works.

Bonus: My Favorite Books List

I will list these books in order of how I would read them if I was just starting my journey into personal development. If you are wondering where to start, trust your gut instinct and go with the first one that grabs your attention, because this is the one your subconscious mind is telling you that you need now.

It might surprise you that none of these books are about trading. Each one of these books, **however,** will be more helpful to your trading than any trading book ever written.

Trading successfully is a high performance sport. Like athletes, to succeed you need the high performance mindset to go along with your skill. Of the two, the former is far more important than the latter.

So pick a book and get started, or get them all. If you want to purchase the complete list all at once, you can visit our website for the link.

Norman Vincent Peale - The Power of Positive Thought

Wallace Wattles - The Science of Getting Rich

Napoleon Hill - Think & Grow Rich

Joseph Murphy - Power of the Subconscious Mind

Maxwell Maltz - Psycho-Cybernetics

CHAPTER 8
DEALING WITH FEAR OF LOSS IN TRADING

When I began my journey into trading in 2001, I expected a smoother sail to my destination. I was optimistic that I would fight through the challenges and reach consistent profitability fairly quickly.

Trading, after all, is the land of promise; a dream job without employees, overhead or a boss to report to. It all sounds so promising, and has the allure to attract people in pursuit of reaching their dreams on their own terms.

In reality, it is one of the hardest jobs in the world - and for the same reasons.

Most of us have been raised with the value of safety, seeking to find something sure without risk. We have been taught to avoid risk, and to play it safe. If you are someone who has a top value of security, you will find trading to be extremely difficult. This business is all about managing risk, which is something very few of us have a chance to learn in the course of life.

But let's take a moment to consider another view of the meaning of risk.

Did you know that every time you eat a piece of chicken you are exposing yourself to the risk of salmonella poisoning? Now that you know this, will you stop eating chicken? Also, there is a one in ten thousand chance you will be injured by a toilet. Will you ever use one again?

Every single day we are exposed to an immense number of risks, which we have to accept if we are planning to get out of bed and do something. In fact, we are accepting risk without an awareness of it.

In trading, there is a risk of losing money. Unlike any of the risks above, **however,** you always know exactly how much is being risked and you get to decide if you want to take it. When you are in a trade, you can also choose to take off the risk. Not only do you know the exact risk exposure, you can manage it with precision.

So trading risk is less risky than eating chicken, or even using the toilet.

A great risk manager is a great trader, and to my knowledge there is no great trader that is not a great risk manager. I know thousands of traders, some with dizzying levels of success. They all manage risk first, and receive a profit in direct proportion to their ability to do so.

So what makes trading so difficult?

Fear. More specifically, the fear of loss. The fear of losing confidence, guaranteed pay checks, failure; all these fears paralyze traders and trigger a cycle of self-sabotage.

You see, for thousands of years fear has kept us safe and is directly responsible for our evolution as a species. Without fear, you wouldn't be here. When you fear something, your cortisol raises and you trigger the fight or flight response. This turns off your logical brain and activates your survival instincts. Trading from this highly emotional state guarantees your failure.

Let me tell you a story of a new trader, named John. His parents were very frugal and always stressed the importance of security. They raised John to attend a good school, get a good job and avoid risk at all cost. Twenty years later, John works as an actuary with a great salary and lives in a small and cozy home with his wife.

Now that his kids have moved on, he decides to give trading a try so he can one day quit his job, and have more time to do the things he loves. John knows it is risky, but decides that his strong rationale will keep him safe and secure. So John reads everything he can online, and develops a strategy that has yielded a lot of success in his practice trading account. He builds the confidence to finally start trading live. As he moves the money from his checking account to his brokerage, he feels a few butterflies. John identifies this as excitement. The next morning he reviews his trading plan, and starts waiting for the conditions to be met to execute his first trade. A few minutes later John finds a suitable trade and enters the market. Immediately after John buys, the position starts to go into the negative territory. But it's okay he thinks to himself, this is part of my plan. The market drops some more, causing a larger loss. John's heart rate escalates, his breathing rate increases and the fear starts to creep up. He starts to think, what if I lose this money? What if I am not smart enough for this? As he thinks this, he notices the market is just one point away from his stop loss. In response, John moves it lower - "it'll come back", he says to himself. Except it doesn't, the price continues to drop. John's heart rate increases even more, he is now sweating and taking shallow, sudden breaths. The fear increases. He can't fail he thinks, and moves his stop loss even lower. The market follows. Fear increases, his heart is pounding and he feels physically ill. The subconscious mind senses that John is in danger, it knows this exact feeling - the same one it felt ten thousand years ago when it was sleeping and a bear was approaching the family cave. The subconscious shuts off the logical factor and forces John to exit the trade, seeking relief from the cause of this emotional rollercoaster. John closes the trade at a loss that is ten times bigger than what was part of his plan. He walks away from the computer, feeling weak, dazed and confused.

Later that night, he reviews his trading plan and thinks to himself, "what the heck happened, I didn't follow my plan and really can't remember why I let this happen". He wonders who did that trade, because it sure as heck didn't feel like it was him. The next day, after a restful sleep he starts the day again by committing to follow the plan. He gets into a trade, it goes against him, he moves his stop lower, panics, and moves it even lower. Another day, another devastating result.

Two weeks later, through repetition of the same pattern, John no longer has any capital in his trading account. He thinks about his parents, what would they have thought if they knew how risky he was acting? John quits trading and goes back to his job as an actuary.

The reason I know this story so well is because I was John. I was not an actuary, but my parents did value security. They feared risk, and so did I when I started trading. If you think back to how you were raised, you'll realize you have picked up those values, too. Until age seven, you are closely studying your parents and adopting their values. This is necessary for survival.

Let me tell you what has happened with Johns around the world when they start trading for the first time.

When your top value is safety and security, risk is a threat. You are concentrated on the negative consequences of taking risk, as a means of avoiding it. When you start trading, you are moving opposite to what you have programmed your subconscious mind to do; avoid risk and create safety. As you lose money, your rational thought is turned off and the system is controlled by the subconscious brain, which takes any action to immediately remove you from the cause of your loss, forcing you to close a trade at an enormous loss. Your rational brain resumes function, creating a massive conflict of what you want versus what happened based on how you programmed your mind.

You want success and the freedom of trading. Yet, your subconscious mind wants you to lose your entire trading account balance so you can stop this risky behavior. Losing money brings safety. If you have no more money, you have no way of going against your values and taking risk. This is what brings failure to well meaning, new traders.

So what happens to John now? If he tries trading again, he will experience a similar result, only this time it will be quicker. The more he tries logically to fix the problem, the quicker it will lead to a complete loss. The problem is not the strategy, it's the subconscious programming you have created for yourself.

But because I was John before, I can share the solution with you. I want you to succeed in this business, and it is my life purpose to help guide you on this journey.

The solution is fairly simple once you know it.

If you value safety and security, you need to disconnect the belief that trading will jeopardize those values. It is not about changing the values, they are created to serve you. You want to shift your beliefs.

If you could work the hours you wanted, when you wanted, be your own boss and get to spend more time doing what you truly love - is this the ultimate safety? Would this give you security for you and your family? And how important is that for you?

Great.

Now if you are eating chicken breasts, or using the toilet, you are currently taking risk. Has this risk jeopardized your safety? Is all risk going to lead to lack of safety and security?

What is riskier, taking risks without a choice; or getting to choose when and how much you risk? So, if you are in control, is it a risk or is it an opportunity?

Now, imagine you choose that you will be using a small portion of your capital for every trade. If this capital can generate the returns that create your dream, what do you call it? Opportunity capital.

That's it - this is all it takes, and everything is fixed now, isn't it?

My world changed when I realized that the only thing there is in life is an opportunity and feedback. When you pair this thinking with your new positive mindset, which you cultivated in the last chapter, you are now an unstoppable dream achieving machine.

From my early years, I was always a day dreamer. I always wanted to create, to improve and to give back. The fears I had for me were internal, the fear of failing. But the more I have failed in my life the more I have learned; there is no failure only feedback.

If you are still skeptical and fearful of losing money, let's take a look at it from another perspective.

If you lose every single dollar you have right now, what would happen? You would still breathe, you would still be loved, you will still have a shelter and food. The worst case scenario in today's environment was the life of kings thousands of years ago. By virtue of you having access to the resources to read this book, you have a lot more than most people. The fact you even had a chance to save up capital and give your dream a try, makes you lucky.

Now, what if you reached your potential and hit your goals? What would happen? In true trading terms, is the risk worth the reward for you? If not, don't even think about trading. The markets are for opportunists.

Let me tell you the real risk of life that very few ever consider, until it is too late.

This story is about a guy named Rick.

Rick worked with a younger colleague, named Steve. Steve was new and eager to establish himself and build his career in a large organization. Rick gave him advice, and mentored him along the way, telling him how to play it safe and how to climb the corporate ladder. Slow and steady. Rick had put his life into his work, sacrificing his personal health. He had ambitions of starting a business when he was younger, but now, he felt it was too late. Besides, he loved his job and was starting to think about his plans for retirement. It wasn't for another fifteen years, but it sure felt like it was going to be an exciting time. Rick was just getting back on his feet after some financial trouble, but he had learned his lessons and was excited for the future.

One day Rick and Steve were reviewing some client documents together, when their boss asked them if they could join him in the meeting room, along with the rest of the team. The boss said the company had faced a setback, and the budget was getting cut. As a result, Rick's role was being eliminated - effective immediately. Steve looked at Rick, and could see he was in shock. His thought is interrupted by three people walking in with boxes, and asking Rick and a few other team members to follow them. Rick never returned.

I know Rick well, as I was Steve.

On that day I learned one of the most important lessons of my life - not taking risk is the biggest risk of all.

I will never forget that day, when my friends and coworkers were walked off the job. They didn't even give them a chance to collect their own belongings. All they got were their jackets, wallets and phones. The rest of their things were packed and shipped to their home.

No way was this ever happening to me, I promised myself.

I have never shared this with anyone, but on that day I mentally resigned from a corporate career and decided I was going to be an entrepreneur. I would work one hundred hour weeks for myself so I didn't have to work a single hour for someone else.

I was making really good money, and while I was young it seemed like the corporate ladder was mine for the climbing. I had the leverage. And I knew that it was only a matter of time before the steps got further apart and were made of more fragile material.

There is one final, and very personal thought I want to share with you on the topic of safety, security and risk.

We all seem to want the same thing; the most amount of satisfaction for the least amount of effort. This is human design, not a coincidence.

But I think back to all the generations before me, which have given their blood, sweat and tears to create this new reality of convenience. We have so much more than anyone has in the past generations. Health care, access to food, ability to choose any job and change careers, ability to connect with almost anyone in the world. Fine dining, vacations, globe trotting in jets. We have everything we need, and the means to get anything we want.

In comparison to where we have come from, to your brothers and sisters in the cave days - your worst case scenario was something they couldn't fathom. It was something they created for us, so why do we feel that we are entitled to safety and security?

For me, I am fine taking risks if it means that I get to be the caveman for future generations.

If I can just leave this world a better place than I found it - it's not a risk, it's an obligation.

Happy Trading!

GEORGE PAPAZOV

CHAPTER 9
LESSONS FROM A PROFESSIONAL TRADER

I f I could travel back in time and talk to myself as a young and ambitious trader in his teens; what would I tell him? These are raw lessons I have learned from battle wounds and over eighteen years of experience in this industry. Through the twists and turns of my turbulent youth to maturation as a man and business owner, I want to share some lessons I picked up along the way.

I will start with a list of general life lessons, then move on to the trading specific ones.

Listen to people who have already achieved what you are after.

Follow your passion, not the profit.

Live in the present, this is where all change happens. The past is gone, the future is not guaranteed. The present is a present.

It's okay to think of yourself first. Take time to satisfy your needs, the more you develop personally the more resources you have to help others with.

Everything is going to be okay. No matter how hard something seems, you will overcome it and eventually the positive outcome will be worth the struggle in retrospect.

Perception is projection. Whatever someone thinks of you is a reflection of themselves. What you think of others is a reflection of yourself. Listen closely.

A person's model of the world is not the person. People are inherently good and are doing the best they can with the resources they have. Understand their model of the world and learn from them, release all judgement.

You have the power to accept or reject. Any thought, idea or opinion that you hear or see is just a message, you can choose to accept it or reject it. Be careful what you accept, because it changes your identity.

Emotions are acceptance. Your emotions are purely your creation. If you are feeling any emotion, it is because you chose to accept and respond to it.

Embrace fears and overcome them. Fears protect me and serve me, I can choose to accept them or overcome them. Most fears are challenges and opportunities.

Everything is temporary. No matter how bad or perfect a moment is, it is temporary. Experience it fully and enjoy it, then release it.

You are borrowing everything, including time. You don't own anything, the only thing there is, is energy. Everything in its current form will be released and transformed back into energy - including you.

Give more than you receive. The goal is to leave this world in a net positive, give more than you receive. Giving is living.

Ego is a condition of lack. When you think you are bigger than something, it is a reflection of an insecurity and comes from a mind state of lack.

The body has the blueprint for perfect health. Everything is meant to be healthy and abundant in its raw form. We program ourselves out of health. Deal with emotional conflict right away.

Live your life like every day is your last. One of these days it will be. Resolve anything that causes you discomfort before going to sleep.

Be responsible for change. Once you achieve big goals it's your responsibility to give back and help others. Standing still and dwelling in success for long periods is an act of lack.

Tell people you love them regularly. Love is the highest emotion you can feel, share it with others and tell them that you love them. You help them and yourself.

There is enough for everyone. The world has infinite potential to create the perfect life for every human being. Humans are born to be abundant.

Rich people are only villains in the movies. You deserve to be rich if you have good intentions and a purpose that will change the world. Money is a resource. Study and model rich people who inspire you instead of alienating them.

It doesn't have to be perfect to be helpful. Perfectionism is a sign of insecurity, if it will help people it doesn't need to be perfect, it's better to exist in current form than not to exist at all.

Even when you fall on your face you are moving forward. There is no failure, only feedback. Think big and swing hard.

If there are no haters you are playing too small. If everyone loves it, it's too small and safe and likely is not helping anyone.

Keep a good circle of friends around, who provide you feedback and help you improve. You become the average of the five people you spend the most time with; so be selective of the company you keep.

Celebrate your successes. It's important to acknowledge the wins in life; no matter how small they may seem, they are worth praising.

Be persistent. Failures and mistakes are part of life. Lebron James doesn't score every shot attempt, you aren't expected to either. Overcome the tough periods and keep moving forward - one foot in front of the other.

Be a student of life, for your entire life. Keep learning new things, accepting new challenges and seeking new information. Success is a process of continuous learning.

Now let's dive into the trading specific lessons I have learned over the years. Some of these won't need an explanation as they are straight forward. I will add some insight and expand on those I think will help you.

These are my own thoughts, and the few that are quotes from other traders are credited to them:

No one knows where the market is going, otherwise it would not exist.

Amateurs chase returns, while professionals manage risk.

Profit in the market is the reward of being an effective risk manager.

To make bigger profits, become a better risk manager.

If you lose less, you will be making more.

Markets are a quantification of collective investor sentiment.

The true price of anything is what someone is willing to pay for it.

Just because you are not long, it doesn't mean you have to be short.

If you were long from below, would you add to your position here? If not, why are you trying to get in now?

The market can always go further than you think, play the side of strength.

A market top or bottom is only apparent after it is no longer a useful trading opportunity.

Markets don't crash from lows, they crash from highs.

I have never lost a trade I haven't taken. Fear of missing out will never help and only hurt you.

The news doesn't matter, what is more important is how that compares to what traders expected.

Once you buy something, you are a seller. - Anthony Drager, a good friend and trader I admire.

Once you sell something, you are a buyer. - Anthony Drager

Limit orders don't move markets, market orders move markets.

Winning trades are not always good trades.

Losing trades are not always bad trades.

Good trades are not always winning trades.

Bad trades are not always losing trades.

Bad trading results don't just happen, you create them.

There are old traders and there are bold traders, but there are very few old, bold traders. - Ed Seykota

Markets are rational. Investors are not. Investors are emotional beings, therefore act irrationally. Markets are the collective sentiment of investors. Therefore, markets are irrational.

If you are not going to get paid when you have an open profit, when will you get paid?

Always get paid, take initial profit and run the balance of the position with no risk.

Scale up your trading size proportionally with your confidence and experience.

When volatility is low, follow the three rules. Trade smaller size. Trade less frequently. Take profits quicker.

When volatility is increasing, increase your trading size and frequency. Match the speed of the market before you shift, and you won't need a clutch.

Stop losses become take profits when you move them above your entry price. Getting stopped out is a good thing when it locks in profit.

When markets crash hard, step on it and make a killing. That's your job. But be humble, kind and respectful, most people are getting hurt. Donate to the cause that is moving the market. I.e. 9/11

The biggest selling happens below levels where long term investors, swing traders and day traders all have their stop losses.

Think before your trade, then focus on executing.

Less is more in this business. Follow only tested studies and stick to as little information as is necessary.

If you are stressed out while you are trading you have an issue. It could be lack of confidence, trading plan or fear.

Practice does not make perfect; it makes permanent. Staying in sim too long creates self-sabotage patterns.

Crude oil can be a crude market for new traders, but a perfect market to expand to.

The market does not care about you. No hard feelings, at least she's honest.

Trading is like surfing, you are in the water watching the waves and deciding which one is right for you.

If you are going to be a successful trader in the future, that means you are already a successful trader now. Appreciate your progress and keep learning.

These are the things I would tell young George, and these are the things I want to pass along to you. The most important thing is to be open to change, and to take on challenges big and scary enough that create your very own learning lessons in life.

When everything is said and done, our one and only lasting contribution to life is the lessons we leave behind, and the change they empower. That is my definition of legacy; serving the world and not the ego. This is a large part of my motivation for creating this book, and I hope it has helped you gain a fresh perspective on trading and your life overall.

Now let's finish off our journey together by creating your very own action plan.

CHAPTER 10
YOUR ACTION PLAN

The most important part about creating a plan is best summarized with the expression: make a plan so you know what won't happen. It's funny, and it's true. A plan would only be perfect if it could guarantee an outcome, and like trading, the only thing that is guaranteed, is that nothing is guaranteed.

Yet, it is important to have a document to guide you through the steps. Something to fall back to when you temporarily get lost. Knowing there's a path ahead helps you find motivation to keep walking through the twists and turns.

In this last chapter, I want to leave you with an action plan that you can use to start your trading journey. Truthfully, I designed this for me - but I will share it with you also. Remember, giving is living.

If I was able to go back in time to 2001, when I first started in this business, I would give myself the following:

STEP 1: SETTING REALISTIC EXPECTATIONS

If you have mismatched expectations, you can feel like you are behind even if you are way ahead. My expectations as a new trader were in dollar terms. How much money I wanted to make. It is important to set your measurement criteria based on learning - do I know more today than yesterday? If yes, repeat.

Tony Robbins once said that most people overestimate what they can achieve in one year, and underestimate what they can achieve in five. I agree with this statement, and I'm living proof. I was disappointed in the first year because I lost money, but in retrospect I was right where I needed to be with the typical development of a trader. Accept the fact that you will be gaining massive knowledge, building your skill, which will be used to generate future returns. Most traders overestimate what they will earn in the first year, and grotesquely underestimate what they can earn in five. Take your time, the foundation you lay in the beginning will need to support a ton of bricks you will be laying on top over time.

What weekdays will I commit to learn?

How many hours is the minimum I will invest each week?

If I'm making $2,000,000 a year in 10 years trading, what is the maximum time I am willing to invest to learn how to do this?

How much income a month do I need to know I'm a good trader?

How much income a month do I want to live my dream life?

How will I spend my time, now that I have achieved my goals?

Good, now visualize a day in your life, see what you see, hear what you hear and feel what you feel. Try it now, do it daily.

STEP 2: FIND A COMMUNITY

Humans are tribal. Social media has made a lot of young billionaires, all because people crave to belong to something. It has also allowed us traders to connect to one another. Who better knows what you are going through than someone who has already gone through it?

Look for a community that matches your expectations, not one that is promising you the fastest route to your ultimate goals. There are no holy grails, fast tracks or magic pills. If there were, you, or I, wouldn't be able to afford them, no offense.

Community gives you feedback, but most importantly lets you master trading by learning from someone and teaching others. The ability to teach something is the highest level of mastery you can reach. Find a community that accepts you, without judgement and criticism. The traders there are successful and willing to help. Most importantly, find a community that trades in a live environment, explaining their thought process, analysis and helps you apply it for yourself.

Here is something you should avoid, as it will destroy your progress. Steer far clear from communities that give you trade signals, when to buy and when to sell. No one cares about your money more than you. Look for opinions, analysis, ideas and even strategies, but never trade signals. Learn to fish, as opposed to waiting for someone to throw you a fish. If they do, you do not want it because they didn't either. My trade is never right for you, and I would never do your trade for the same reason. We all have our own style, find yours. Be patient.

I've put together a few questions to ask yourself as you search for your tribe.

What is the identity of the community that you want to belong to?

Are there professional traders who I want to learn from?

Is this a supportive environment or one of ego and showmanship?

Can I ask questions safely, without being made to feel new?

Use your gut on this one: Can I trust this community?

Are there people in this community who have started at the beginning and have become successful?

What are other people saying and can I interact with them?

These questions will give you a good starting point.

My opinion is that we have the best online trading community in the world at TRADEPRO Academy. Obviously, I am what some would call biased, but if you do your homework and answer the questions above you'll quickly find that you agree. We have massive success stories, and you can be the next. Our entire community will help you get there.

No matter what you choose, it's important to get into a community as quickly as possible. I wish these existed when I started.

STEP 3: BE A SPONGE

Once you've found a community, the rest of the process is easy. It is your job to learn everything, and anything. At this point, you aren't looking for a strategy, indicators or anything in particular. You are just absorbing everything. It doesn't even matter what you will be trading at this point, all that matters is you are learning about markets. In today's age, markets are so interconnected that if you learn about one you know a lot about others. Market structure and price action are similar across all assets.

How long should you be a sponge for? For the rest of your life. Trading is a business of constant learning and growth. The moment you think you know it all, your performance is at its peak.

STEP 4: CREATE A BUSINESS PLAN (TRADING STRATEGY)

Put together a trading strategy. This is like a business plan, which includes when you will take an opportunity, how much risk you will accept and how you will manage it. You should start with just one strategy, but as time progresses and you gain more experience you will end up having multiple strategies for multiple markets.

This process warrants its own book, but the good news is we have the template available in our community and the resources to start creating.

Like a true business plan, there is a lot to consider in putting one together. This is something you want to spend time on, as it will be the action steps to achieve your goals. There is no need to rush, and you know it is done when it feels right.

STEP 5: FORM A FEEDBACK LOOP

Remember the community part? This is where it is vital. Having a sounding board to bounce ideas off of, and to have someone help you review your plan is essential. The feedback of someone who has walked your path before is critical, because they know what you may not, and could give you considerations you have never considered. As a new trader, you don't know what you don't know. Listen to feedback, be critical about it, come up with more questions and be a sponge. I have personally learned about new strategies, ideas and tools from our members that have helped me optimize my performance. I love our community.

STEP 6: WHEN TO GO LIVE

If you have to ask this question, the answer is not now. You want to feel confident about your plan, and have some experience executing. I'm a firm believer that you should also not overstay your time in a simulated account. If you have a plan, have tested it and feel good, it's time to try it live. The important part is to start with a smaller scale, as small as possible. There is no need to max out your trade size with a new plan, as a new trader. Flying by the seat of your pants is not a good idea. In this phase, you are still in the feedback, adjustment and learning phase. The goal is not to make millions of dollars, it is to not lose - protect your capital. If you are learning while trading with real money, and breaking even - you are doing phenomenal at this stage. Once you experience the emotions of managing risk, and improve your skills with screen time, you can start to scale up. Start small, increase and decrease size proportionally to success and experience. Remember, have fun, you are in the early stages of living your dream life. Keep doing the visualization from step one daily.

STEP 7: ACCOUNTABILITY PARTNER

As you develop your trading personality and style, you will naturally gravitate towards people with a similar approach. You will find a friend in the community that you resonate with. Build a relationship and help one another grow. Help them, and be helped by them. For constant growth, I always encourage our members to find someone that is also different, you can learn a lot from different perspectives. It's a balance between continuing to do what you are, and constantly searching for ways to improve.

STEP 8: REVIEW, REVISE AND GROW

This step will continue for as long as you trade, which will hopefully be a very long time (forever). By the time you get to this step, you will know so much that it will be intuitive for you. Within a community of traders, you eventually develop to the point of unconscious competence - you don't realize how much you know. But no matter how much you think you know, there is always more to know if you want to continue to prosper and grow.

That is all. I really hope you loved reading this book as much as I did writing it.

It is not a goodbye, as I'm sure I'll be seeing you in our community. I am excited to introduce you to the rest of our TRADEPROs.

I send you an abundance of love, joy, happiness and health to you and your beautiful family.

Always have fun; laugh, learn and earn.

And remember, giving is living.

Sayonara.

Made in the USA
Coppell, TX
16 January 2020